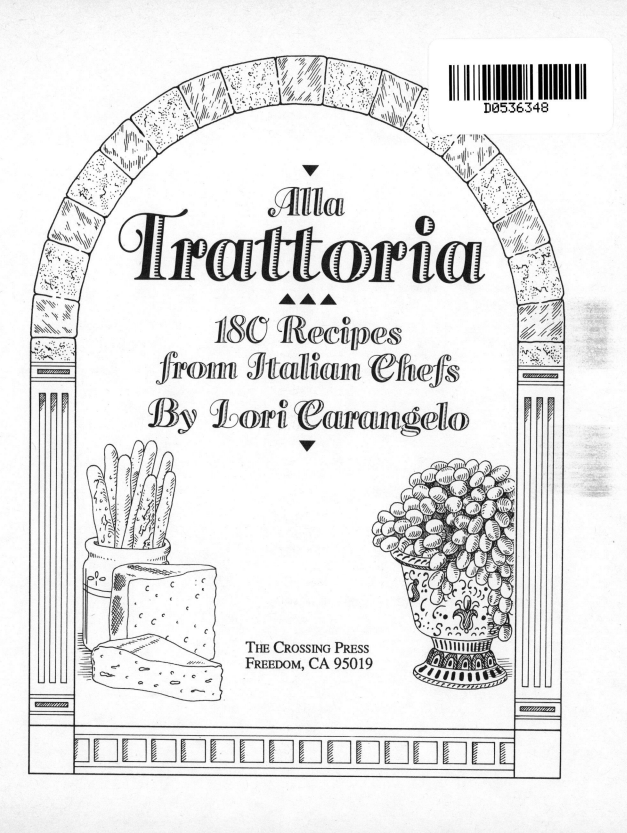

Alla Trattoria

180 Recipes from Italian Chefs

By Lori Carangelo

THE CROSSING PRESS
FREEDOM, CA 95019

Cover art and design by Angelini & Angelini
Interior art by Angelini & Angelini

Printed in the U.S.A.

Cataloging-in-Publication Data

Carangelo, Lori.
    Alla trattoria : more than 180 recipes from Italian chefs /
by Lori Carangelo.
          p.   cm.
    Includes index.
    ISBN 0-89594-450-2 (paper) -- ISBN 0-89594-451-0 (cloth)
    1. Cookery, Italian.   I. Title.
TX723 . C2837 1991
641 . 5945--dc20   91-6555
                                       CIP

Contents

Preface

I went to Italy to search for my roots. Somehow, all of my research came to be bound up in food, because Italians love to cook and share good food. While researching my grandfather Camillo Dolceacqua's birthplace in Dolceacqua, Liguria, I found my relatives and was wined and dined beyond my wildest culinary fantasies.

Upon visiting my grandmother Maria Grazia Benevento's birthplace on the Amalfi Coast in southern Italy's Campania region, I collected recipes for their world famous pizzas and pastas. One very memorable meal was served at Zeffirino's famous restaurant in Genoa, a favorite of both Pope John Paul II and Frank Sinatra. Indeed, everywhere I traveled, I collected recipes that I've made again and again.

When I returned home I had more than an appreciation of my ancestors and the lives they led. I came home with the basis for this book—prize recipes from noteworthy restaurants in Italy. Later I added to my collection with recipes from Italian restaurants from as far away as Australia, and as close to home as the family restaurant in town.

The Italian cooking I love is firmly rooted to the land. Even in the most cosmopolitan Roman restaurant, the sumptuous menu is based on the classic cuisine of simple farmers' kitchens.

The recipes in this book are the same as those carefully prepared in the neighborhood trattoria each night—the sort of place that has a menu always posted in the front window or just inside the door, next to a sign that reads *"Produzione Propria,"* which means homemade.

The recipes remind me of the numerous times I ended a day making new friends with a relaxing meal at a local trattoria. In Italy, trattorias are less fancy than *ristorantes*, and more expensive and formal than *tavola calda* (hot tables) or *roticcerie* (grills). We always tried to sample the best eating of each region—*tagliatelle con pesto* in Genoa, *lasagna verdi* in Bologna, *bistecca alla Fiorentina* in Florence, *saltimbocca* in Rome, pizza in Naples. And each meal was accompanied by a local wine. More often than not, the food was simple, honest, and appealing. There were no mystery sauces or secret ingredients to mask the flavor of fresh foods carefully prepared.

I hope you will enjoy this cook's tour as much as I did. And I hope you'll have the opportunity to sample these wonderful dishes not only in your own kitchen, but in the famous restaurants where they are made and served with love.

Measurements and Approximations

Despite most restaurants' eagerness to contribute their recipes to this book, the process of translation was often difficult. It was not so much due to the language barrier, but to the Italians' indifference to precise measurements. Just as my Italian grandmother created gastronomic wonders with a handful of this and a pinch of that, so do many master chefs. They are guided by feel, not by the measuring cup. One comes to know, from the love of cooking and selecting the freshest natural ingredients, how much will feed how many, how much is enough to create the desired flavor and result. But for the novice, I have translated and elaborated upon nearly all the recipes contained here. Measurements in grams and kilograms were converted to pounds, and then to cups. Don't be afraid to approximate; it's very difficult to ruin an Italian dish. The result depends upon the excellence of the ingredients, and that varies from one tomato to the next. Therefore, the same recipe may not turn out exactly the same every time. Only you can judge whether the pasta is *al dente* (firm to the tooth) or whether more salt is needed. The amount of sauce, the number of servings—it's all up to you and your guests.

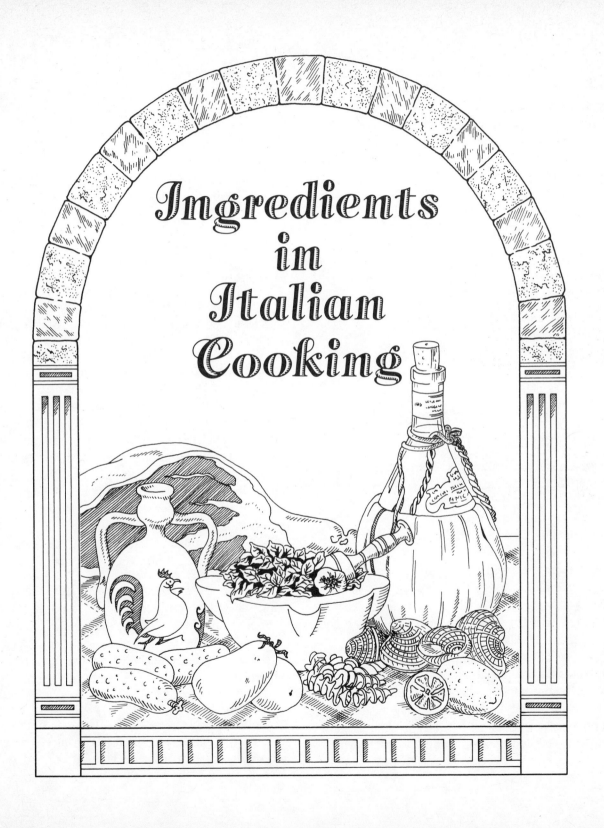

Ingredients in Italian Cooking

*I*f your only exposure to Italian cooking has been in those Italian-American restaurants where every dish is smothered in a heavily spiced tomato sauce, you may have the wrong idea of what Italian cooking is all about. Italian cooking is about fresh ingredients, carefully prepared to bring out the essential flavor and character of the ingredients at hand.

Most of the ingredients called for in this cookbook are readily available in the States. Some ingredients, such as fresh mozzarella, you are most likely to find by seeking out specialty producers. And some, such as crimini mushrooms, are most likely obtained dried through importers. Mail order sources of Italian foods are listed in the back of this book.

Here is a listing and discussions of some of the ingredients you'll want to have on hand.

Garlic and Onions in Italian Cooking

Pliny, the Roman historian, lists 61 medicinal uses for garlic. It is said to cure colds, warts, fainting spells, and insect and snake bites. It is said to stop vampires, improve circulation, alleviate high blood pressure, ward off the evil eye, repel fleas, and cause hair to grow.

A number of folk sayings indicate the importance of garlic and onions in Italian cuisine: "Peace and happiness begin where garlic is used in cooking," and "Banish garlic from the kitchen and the pleasure of eating flies with it."

A fundamental procedure in a vast number of Italian dishes is sauteing onion or garlic or both in hot fat before adding other ingredients. This provides background flavor, which may be faint or pronounced, sweet or pungent, depending on how lightly or deeply the onion and garlic are browned.

Garlic colors more quickly than onion, so if a recipe calls for both, saute the onion first, then add the garlic when the onion becomes a light gold color. The stronger or darker the browning, the stronger the flavor.

Garlic gives all its flavor to the sauce when it is cut so finely it is almost mashed. Removing the tiny green germ in the center of the clove before cooking will eliminate the strong garlic smell if that is objectionable to you.

Herbs and Spices of Italy

Beyond onion and garlic, several herbs and spices, all readily available in the United States, lend flavor to Italian dishes. Here is a listing of them.

Basil (*Basilico*). A member of the mint family, basil has a distinctive, spicy aroma. Fresh, it may very well be the best of all herbs to use to flavor tomatoes and tomato sauce. In Italian cooking it is associated with the region of Liguria, the home of pesto, the aromatic paste of basil, olive oil, Parmesan cheese, garlic, and pine nuts. Basil retains the most flavor when it is cut and added to a dish at the last moment. The fresh leaves can be preserved by covering with oil (preferably olive oil) in a lidded jar and refrigerating or freezing. Dried basil loses a good deal of its pungency.

Bay Leaf (*Lauro*). A native of the Mediterranean, the stiff green leaves were used to crown Olympic champions. Today, the bay laurel leaf is used to flavor soups, casseroles, stews, and roasts. The leaf is usually removed before the dish is served.

Cinnamon (*Cannella*). This ancient spice is used primarily in sweet dishes, but it is occasionally added to meat and garnishes in places where the Middle Eastern influences is felt.

Fennel (*Finocchio*). Fennel is grown extensively throughout Italy. A member of the carrot family, the bulb of this plant has an anise flavor and is used whole or sliced, as a cooked vegetable or raw in salads. The leaves are used in sauces, mayonnaise, and egg and fish dishes. The seeds flavor sausages, cooked meats, dried figs, and cookies.

Italian Parsley (*Prezzemolo*). This is a flat-leafed variety used to flavor soups, stews, salads, and serves as a garnish to these and many other dishes. It is milder in flavor than the curly leaf parsley familiar to most Americans.

Marjoram (*Maggiorana*). Closely related to oregano, marjoram is a sweet, aromatic herb used in soups, stews, and vegetable and fish dishes.

Mint (*Menta*). Used with vegetables, soups, salads, fish, and fowl, mint should be used sparingly since it is very aromatic. Mint is characteristic of the cooking of southern Italy, which was influenced by the cooking of the Middle East.

Nutmeg (*Noce Moscata*). A pinch of nutmeg is used to flavor spinach, mushrooms, ravioli, and cheese dishes. Nutmeg is always freshly grated in Italian cooking. The packaged ground nutmeg cannot compare in flavor and aroma to the fresh.

Oregano (*Origano*). This herb, the wild variety of marjoram, is the herb most closely associated with Italian cooking in America. The unmistakable flavor of oregano is found in pizza, sauces, and casseroles. Oregano is one of the few herbs that does not lose flavor when dried.

Pepper (*Pepe*). Peppercorns were used as far back as the Greek and Roman periods, and their popularity in northern Europe made the spice merchants of Venice and Genoa quite rich. Black and white peppercorns come from the same berry; the white is picked when the berry is almost ripe, the black is picked when the berry is still unripe. Both are then dried. Black peppercorns have the stronger flavor, but white is preferable for some dishes.

Rosemary (*Rosmario*). A perennial shrub that grows wild by the sea, rosemary has leaves that resemble small needles. It is used most often with roasted meats, particularly lamb, chicken, and pork. This is a very aromatic herb and both the fresh and dried herb should be used sparingly.

Saffron (*Zafferano*). Saffron lends a distinctive flavor and yellow color to foods. Saffron is very expensive as it is the collected pollen of the crocus flower, so it is used sparingly. (Something like 40,000 flowers are required to make 1 pound of the spice.) It is available as a powder or in threads (the stigmas of the flower). The most economical way to use saffron is to steep threads in tepid water for a few minutes, strain and add the liquid to the dish for color and taste. *Risotto alla Milanese* is a classic dish enhanced by saffron.

Sage (*Salvia*). Once established in a garden, this herb blooms year after year. A member of the mint family, sage is used to flavor veal, liver, and sausage.

Salt (*Sale*). The salt generally used in Italy is sea salt, extracted from evaporated sea water. The fruity flavor improves the simplest dish. Sea salt can be obtained in many supermarkets, as well as in natural foods stores.

When adding salt, bear in mind that some of the ingredients already present, or to be added later in the dish, may be salty. This is often the case with sauces for pasta. Romano sprinkled on top of a spaghetti dinner is saltier than fresh Parmesan; commercial brands of Parmesan are saltier tasting than either fresh Parmesan or fresh Romano. If the sauce contains prosciutto, sausages, anchovies, capers, or cheese, you may need to hold back some of the salt you add to the water in which you boil the pasta. But understand that adding salt to pasta at the table is seldom as effective as adding salt to the water in which the pasta was cooked.

Prolonged contact with salt draws out moisture—you may want to do this sometimes, as when cooking eggplant, but you definitely do not want to lose any precious moisture from veal scaloppine, chicken breasts, or thin slices of beef. In sauteing these, do not add any salt until they are almost completely cooked.

Salted batter diminishes the crispness of deep-fried foods, but totally unsalted fried food can never be adequately corrected at the table.

In many recipes, lemon juice is the perfect substitute for salt, especially for people on salt-restricted diets.

Thyme (*Timo*). This easy-to-grow herb with its mint-like aroma is used in stuffings, soups, casseroles, and beans.

Vanilla (*Vaniglia*). To flavor desserts, keep a vanilla bean (which is expensive) in ordinary sugar to give additional flavor.

Italian Cheeses

Italians have been making cheese for thousands of years. The cheese that comes from the Alps is very different from that which comes from the Po Valley, the Abruzzi, or from the hot South. There is creamy Bel Paese, and blue-striped Gorgonzola, sharp sheep's cheese from Rome, and the hard, flaky Parmesan cheese which is made from whey and, when freshly grated, is used to perk up soups, sauces, and pasta dishes.

The following cheeses are available in the U.S. in Italian markets and specialty food stores, if not at your supermarket.

Asiago. This cheese dates back to the Middle Ages, though it was scarcely known outside of the Veneto region until relatively recently. When young, asiago is a semi-soft slicing cheese, great for pastas and pizza. Aged asiago can be grated and is sometimes used as a substitute for Parmesan cheese by those watching their diets.

Bel Paese. A semi-soft, very mild cheese made from cow's milk. It is used as a table cheese, but its melting qualities make it suitable for cooking.

Caciocavallo. Similar to provolone cheese. It originally came from the southern provinces but is now also made in northern Italy. It is mild, has a spicy tang when young, and is used mostly as a table cheese, although it hardens as it matures and can then be grated.

Fontina. A fairly firm cheese, similar to Gruyère in texture, with tiny holes on the surface. Not only is it indispensable in preparing fondue, but it is an excellent table cheese. The taste is slightly sweet, with a nutty flavor. Don't confuse Italian fontina with Danish fontina; the two are not really similar.

Gorgonzola. A rich, creamy, blue-green veined cheese made from whole cow's milk. It can be mild (*dolce*) or sharp (*piccante*). It is used as a table cheese and is particularly tasty over pasta.

Mascarpone. A rich, fresh cream cheese that spreads easily. It can be eaten sprinkled with sugar and/or cocoa powder for a treat. In this country, marscapone is newly popular prepared in tiramisu, which is made with sponge cake soaked in brandy and espresso and layered with a mascarpone custard.

Mozzarella. Originally made from water buffalo milk, most mozzarella is now made from cow's milk, although some buffalo milk mozzarella can be found in Italian specialty food shops. A bland, smooth cheese, it is prized for its melting qualities in lasagna, pizza, and other baked dishes; sliced cold in salads and sandwiches, it has a mild, nutty flavor. Fresh mozzarella is far superior to the packaged cheese one can buy in any supermarket. Fresh mozzarella is also very perishable and should be used within 2 to 3 days after purchasing. Smoked mozzarella keeps a bit longer.

Parmesan (*Parmigiano*). Made from cow's milk, good Parmesan is straw-colored, crumbly, and mellow, but salty, in flavor. The best and most expensive is Parmigiano-Reggiano (from Parma, Italy). Aged Parmesan is grated and served over pasta, in soups, salads, and many other dishes; it is best when freshly grated. In Italy, when this cheese is very fresh and moist, it is eaten as a table cheese.

Pecorino. A medium sharp cheese made from sheep's or goat's milk. Pecorino Romano, a hard cheese that is aged for 8 months, is used alone in dishes or combined with Parmesan.

Provolone. A hard, but creamy, cheese made from cow's milk, provolone can be mild or sharp, fresh or smoked. It melts easily and can be grated or sliced.

Ricotta. Ricotta resembles a smooth cottage cheese and can be made from either cow's or goat's milk. Actually it isn't made from fresh milk at all; ricotta is made from whey, the liquid by-product of cheese production. Fresh ricotta is used in cooking, but it can also be a table cheese; it is used as a filling of both pasta and pastries, including cannoli.

Meats

Many of the recipes call for prosciutto as a flavoring agent. This is a very delicately flavored, high-quality cured ham. There are several different types of prosciutto, and all are cured with a similar formula, but aged for varying lengths of time. The prosciutto considered best is from Parma (Parma hams). These are taken from young pigs raised on the whey that is the by-product of making Parmesan cheese. Only recently has the U.S. government allowed Italian prosciutto to be once again imported into this country after a ban of 20 years. (There were questions about the meat's safety as an uncooked product.) Look for it in specialty food stores and expect to pay a premium price.

Pancetta is often referred to as Italian bacon. It is the same cut as American bacon, but the flavor of this cured and air-dried meat is different. Pancetta can be used instead of prosciutto in a recipe.

Oil

It's hard to even imagine Italian cooking without olive oil, although olive oil was once found mainly in the South. When added uncooked to a dish, it supplies a marvelous fruity fragrance. It also lends flavor to any dish cooked with it.

There are several grades of olive oil. The finest olive oils, with the richest flavor and aroma and the deepest green coloring are virgin olive oils. Virgin olive oil is extracted from the first pressing of olives. There is extra virgin olive oil, with a maximum acidity of 1 percent; superfine virgin olive, fine virgin olive oil, and virgin olive oil have increasing amounts of acidity (up to 3.5 percent). These oils are all suitable for using in dishes that require no cooking. Pure olive oil is a blend of refined oil and virgin oil, and it is suitable for use in cooking.

Flour

Most of the recipes in this book require all-purpose flour, even the recipes for making pasta. Although good dried pasta is made from semolina flour or durum wheat, fresh pasta is lighter and richer because it contains eggs. So fresh pasta is usually made with all-purpose flour, which contains a percentage of hard wheat (durum) flour.

A few recipes call for a soft Italian flour. For these recipes, use cake flour or pastry flour. If you use all-purpose flour, use a little less flour than the recipe suggests.

Antipasti

*A*ntipasto, literally "before the meal" (not "before the pasta" as it is often translated), is a dish served before the meal, as hors d'ouevres. Antipasto is not usually served at home, but there are some restaurants that are famed for their antipasti tables, with as many as 60 different dishes to tantalize. The average trattoria offers an antipasto consisting of a few pieces of salami, a slice of prosciutto with olives, pickled vegetables, or mushrooms. Although an antipasto dish is usually considered to be an appetizer, many antipasti are generous enough to make an entire meal, by American standards. Both the individual ingredients and the traditional combinations are listed here. These foods are available in Italian markets and specialty food stores, if not at your supermarket.

Sausages

Cappocollo—Smoked pork
Chipolata—Small pork and rice sausages ("little fingers")
Mortadella—Original Bolognese pork sausage flavored with peppercorns, pistachios, wine, sugar, and olives. This smooth mix (pounded in a mortar, hence its name) is what has come to be known as bologna or baloney
Salsicca secca—Dry and peppery pork sausage

Salami

Various salt-cured pork sausages. Salami are made throughout Italy; the seasonings, sizes, and smoothness of the grind varies from region to region.

Calabrese—A red hot salami from southern Italy
Campagnole—A rough-textured, spicy, peasant salami

Cotechino—Large, cooked pork salami
Cotto—Soft, cooked sandwich-size salami
Genoa—Veal and pork seasoned salami
Milano—Beef and pork seasoned salami
Pepperoni—Small dry salami-like sausage, sweet or hot
Soppressata—Oval, flat salami; peppery, gingery, very garlicky in flavor

Ham

Prosciutto—Thin-sliced, raw cured ham

Vegetables

Caponata, any dried bean or chick-pea salad, marinated or pickled beets or artichoke hearts, green or ripe olives, radishes, celery or carrots, fennel or celery hearts, pickled hot green or red peppers, pimientos in oil, cherry tomatoes.

Cheeses

Provolone, mozzarella, and gorgonzola are cheeses featured in antipasto dishes.

Antipasto Combinations

Calamari al Pesto—Squid with pesto
Calamari Ripieni—Stuffed squid
Capitone sotto Aceto—Eels in marinade
Caponata alla Siciliana—Eggplant relish
Carciofi alla Romana—Artichokes, Roman style
Carciofi Ripieni—Stuffed artichokes
Carciofini—Artichoke hearts
Cipolle Ripieni—Stuffed onions
Cipolline alla Zaferano—Pearl onions in saffron
Cozze en Salsa Verde—Mussels in green sauce
Fagiole con Peperoni—Beans with sweet peppers
Funghi al Limone—Pickled mushrooms
Funghi Marinata—Marinated mushrooms

Funghi Ripieni—Stuffed mushrooms
Giardiniera—Pickled vegetable salad
Melanzane Marinate—Marinated eggplant
Muscoli alla Marinara—Mussels in marinara sauce
Peperoni Rossi Ripieni—Stuffed red bell peppers
Peperoni Verdi Ripieni—Stuffed green bell peppers
Peperonconi—Small green peppers pickled in vinegar
Petto di Vitello Farcito—Stuffed breast of veal
Prosciutto e Melone—Italian ham and melon
Pomodori con Olive—Tomatoes with olives
Pomodori Ripieni—Stuffed tomatoes
Scampi all'Aglio—Shrimp in garlic sauce
Scarola Ripieni—Stuffed escarole
Torta Rustica di Carne—Small meat pie, country-style
Trippa alla Friuliana—Tripe, Friuli style
Trippa di Borgataro—Tripe, Borgataro style
Trotta en Carpione—Pickled trout
Vongole all'Oregano—Clams with oregano
Zucchini Fritti—Fried zucchini
Zucchini Ripieni—Stuffed zucchini
Zucchini Scapece—Minted zucchini

Other Antipasti

Bruschetta—Thick slices of toasted bread seasoned with garlic, oil, salt, and pepper.
Carpaccio—Very thin medallions of raw beef arrayed on a platter, lightly glossed with olive oil and decorated with anchovy filets, roasted slivers of green pepper, and scatterings of capers (can be served as an appetizer or first course).
Crostini—Fingers of bread baked with mozzarella, anchovies, tomato, oregano, salt, and pepper.
Spiedini—Cheese skewers (usually mozzarella, bread, and anchovies).

Carciofi alla Venezia Giulia

(Artichokes Venezia Giulia Style)
Yield: 6 servings

The artichokes for this recipe must be young; they should not yet have formed a "choke."

16 small artichokes
Juice of 1 lemon
6 to 8 tablespoons fresh bread crumbs
1 garlic clove, minced
2 to 3 sprigs parsley, finely chopped
1 cup olive oil
Salt and pepper to taste

Prepare each artichoke by cutting off the stalk (the artichoke should stand easily on its base) and by trimming off the tough lower leaves. Carefully open out the remaining leaves. Soak the artichokes in water to cover with the lemon juice for 15 minutes.

Combine the bread crumbs, garlic, parsley, and 2 to 3 tablespoons of the olive oil to make a stuffing. Season with salt and pepper.

Drain the artichokes and push the stuffing in between the leaves. Arrange the artichokes upright in a pan just large enough to hold them. Pour over the remaining oil, and add enough water to come halfway up the sides of the artichokes. Cover the pan, bring the water to a boil, and simmer until the artichokes are tender, about 30 minutes. Add more water if necessary during the cooking. Remove the artichokes from the water, drain, and serve hot.

Emilio Pesaro
Adriatico
Grado, Italy

Pane con Formaggio

(Bread with Cheese)
Yield: 4 servings

1/2 cup butter
1 teaspoon minced garlic
1 small loaf French bread
1 to 2 cups freshly grated mozzarella cheese
4 teaspoons chopped fresh basil

Preheat the oven to 450°F.

In a small saucepan, melt the butter. Add the garlic and gently simmer for about 2 minutes.

Slice the bread in half horizontally; then cut each half into 4 to 6 pieces. Brush each piece of bread with the garlic butter and arrange on a baking sheet. Sprinkle with grated mozzarella and basil. Toast in the oven for 3 to 5 minutes, or until the cheese is melted and bubbly. Serve hot.

Elsie McFarland
Caro Rico
Portland, Oregon

Fagioli Toscanelli al Caviale

(Tuscan Beans with Caviar)
Yield: 4 servings

1/2 pound dry white beans
3/4 cup extra virgin olive oil
2 large garlic cloves, minced
1 teaspoon chopped fresh sage
1 tablespoon caviar
1/3 cup fresh lemon juice
Salt and pepper to taste

Soak the beans overnight in water to cover by 2 inches. The next day drain the beans and add fresh water, covering the beans by 2 inches. Bring the beans to a boil and simmer until tender. Rinse and add the olive oil, garlic, sage, caviar, lemon juice, and salt and pepper. Mix gently. Allow to marinate for at least 30 minutes (preferably longer) before serving. Serve at room temperature.

Mario Di Fillipis
Buca di San Francesco
Arezzo, Italy

Parmesan Pie with Truffles

Yield: 6 to 8 servings

In the autumn, truffles (tartufi) are plentiful in northern Italy where this recipe originated.

White truffles, thinly sliced
Parmesan cheese (aged less than 1 year), diced
Olive oil

Heat the oven to 350°F.

Grease a baking dish. Cover the bottom with a single layer of truffles. Add a layer of Parmesan, another layer of truffles, and a final layer of Parmesan. Sprinkle with olive oil and bake for a few minutes, just long enough to soften the cheese and bind it with the truffles.

Variation

Start with a layer of polenta, then alternate layers of truffles and Parmesan.

Bob Milligani
Lancaster, California

Panzarotti

(Fried Cheese-Stuffed Ravioli)
Yield: 6 servings

Filling

1 cup diced fresh mozzarella cheese
2 eggs
5 tablespoons grated Parmesan cheese
Salt to taste
1/4 pound salami or Parma ham (prosciutto), diced (optional)

Ravioli

2 1/2 cups all-purpose flour
1/2 cup olive oil
2 egg yolks
Salt
Vegetable oil for frying

To make the filling, combine the mozzarella in a bowl with the eggs, Parmesan, salt, and salami. Mix thoroughly. Set aside while you make the dough.

To make the dough, sift the flour into a mound on a pastry board or into a bowl. Make a well in the center. Add the oil, a pinch of salt, the egg yolks, and about 1 tablespoon lukewarm water. Mix well. Knead to a firm dough. If the dough is too dry, add water; if too wet, add flour. When it is smooth and elastic, put it in a lightly floured bowl, cover, and allow to rest for about 30 minutes. Roll the dough into a thin sheet; then cut it into circles about 2 1/2 inches in diameter. Put a teaspoon of the filling mixture on each circle of dough, fold the circle in half, and seal the edges with a fork.

Deep fry the panzarotti a few at a time until crisp and golden brown. Drain. Serve very hot.

Gianni Piccinni
Giacondo
Cosenza, Italy

Fried Mozzarella Marinara

Yield: 2 to 4 servings

1 cup dry bread crumbs
Salt and pepper to taste
1/2 cup grated Parmesan cheese
1/2 pound mozzarella cheese, cut in pieces 3 inches by 2 inches by 1/2 inch
1 egg, beaten
1/3 cup all-purpose flour
Vegetable oil
Approximately 1 cup Marinara Sauce (see page 42)

Mix the bread crumbs with the salt and pepper and 2 tablespoons of the Parmesan cheese.

Dip the cheese slices into the beaten egg, then into the flour, then into the seasoned bread crumbs, turning to coat all sides. Place the pieces of breaded cheese in a single layer on a plate and chill for 30 minutes.

Heat 1/2 inch of oil in a large, heavy pan. Fry the cheese pieces until lightly browned on one side, then turn and brown on the other side. Take care not to overcook or the cheese will toughen. Drain the cheese pieces on paper towels.

Serve the fried mozzarella with a dish of heated Marinara Sauce for dipping and the rest of the Parmesan cheese for sprinkling.

Richard Cicchi
Santa Barbara, California

Verze Ripiene

(Stuffed Cabbage)
Yield: 8 to 10 servings

1 large head cabbage (savoy is recommended)
1 pound ground pork
1 cup cooked white rice
1/2 cup chopped onions
1/4 cup chopped fresh parsley
1/2 cup grated Romano or Parmesan cheese
1/4 teaspoon dried oregano
2 1/2 teaspoons salt
3/4 teaspoon freshly ground black pepper
3 cups tomato puree
1 bay leaf

Wash the cabbage head, place it in a large pot, and cover with water. Bring to a boil; then simmer for 10 minutes. Drain. Let the cabbage stand until it is cool enough to handle. Remove 24 large leaves.

Mix together the pork, rice, onions, parsley, cheese, oregano, 1 1/2 teaspoons of the salt, and 1/2 teaspoon of the pepper. Place a heaping teaspoon of the mixture on each leaf, turn in the sides, and carefully roll up. (If any meat mixture is leftover, make more meat rolls or make meatballs.)

Preheat the oven to 350°F. Arrange the rolls in a greased casserole or baking dish. Add the tomato sauce, the remaining salt and pepper, and the bay leaf. Cover and bake for 1 1/2 hours. Taste for seasoning, discard the bay leaf, and serve hot.

Bob Milligani
Lancaster, California

Scarole Ripieni

(Stuffed Escarole)
Yield: 6 to 8 servings

2 cups fresh bread crumbs
1/4 cup grated Romano cheese
1/4 cup grated Parmesan cheese
2 garlic cloves, minced
2 tablespoons raisins
2 tablespoons pine nuts
1 tablespoon chopped fresh parsley
Dash pepper
2 small heads escarole
1 tablespoon olive oil

To make the stuffing, combine the bread crumbs, Romano cheese, Parmesan cheese, 1 clove minced garlic, the raisins, pine nuts, parsley, and pepper in a mixing bowl. Set aside.

Leaving the heads intact, spread the leaves of the escarole gently and wash thoroughly. Turn each head upside down and drain well. Open the head, spreading the leaves until the center is exposed. Place half the stuffing in the center of each head. Bring the escarole leaves up over the filling and tie with string.

In a large saucepan, heat the olive oil. Add the remaining clove of garlic and saute until golden. Add 1 cup of water and the escarole. Cover tightly and cook over medium heat for about 8 minutes. Turn the escarole over. Cook, covered, for 5 more minutes or until the escarole is tender.

To serve, slice the escarole crosswise.

"C. C." Gatta
Indian Wells, California

The Italian cook's repertoire includes a rich assortment of soups. The lighter, less filling soups (*minestra*) with a clear broth base (*broda*) make an excellent first course. Sometimes the broth base will be slightly thickened with egg and perhaps grated Parmesan cheese. The distinct shapes of the vegetables and pasta or rice are retained in these soups.

For a lunch or dinner entree, there are the more substantial soups (*zuppa*), brimming with meat, poultry, fish, or vegetables. Often these are served ladled over a piece of bread or toast. This tradition has its roots in medieval times, when servants made soups from the leavings of the noble men and women. In those days, large slices of bread were used instead of plates to hold food—so the plates, ladened with leftovers, were tossed into the pot, along with water and herbs. The result: zuppa!

Minestrone alla Genovese

(Minestrone Soup, Genoa-Style)
Yield: 10 to 12 servings

This soup is a classic: a green minestrone in a clear soup base. The color comes from the addition of pesto at the last moment.

1 pound ham
1 pound chicken parts (wings, backs, neck)
1/4 pound sliced prosciutto
2 cups peeled and diced potato
2 cups sliced celery
4 small zucchini, diced
1/2 cup sliced leeks
1 pound Italian green beans, sliced in 2-inch pieces
1/2 cup uncooked ditalini
1 cup freshly shelled or frozen peas
3 to 4 cups shredded cabbage
About 2 tablespoons salt
1 cup Pesto (see page 28)

In a large kettle, combine 4 quarts water, the ham, chicken, and prosciutto, and bring to a boil. Reduce the heat, cover, and simmer for 2 hours. Strain and reserve the stock, discarding the meat and bones.

Bring the stock to a boil. Add the potatoes, reduce the heat, cover, and simmer for 10 minutes. Add the celery, zucchini, leeks, green beans, and ditalini. Simmer, uncovered, for 4 to 5 minutes. Add salt to taste.

To serve, pour the soup into individual soup bowls. Top each serving with a generous dollop of pesto.

Lori Carangelo
Indian Wells, California

Zuppa Francesca

Yield: 1 serving

An old dish cooked by Franciscan Friars in the 1800s.

1 tomato
2 garlic cloves
1 teaspoon minced fresh parsley
1 tablespoon olive oil
6 fresh basil leaves
Salt to taste
Pinch dried thyme
1 egg yolk
4 slices toasted bread

Dip the tomato into boiling water for about 10 seconds. Cool and peel. Make a cut at the bottom of the tomato, and wedge in 1 clove of garlic.

Heat the olive oil and parsley in a saucepan until the oil turns golden brown, about 3 minutes. Add the tomato and fry it for 2 minutes; then pour some water into the saucepan to almost cover the tomato. Add the basil and salt, and let simmer for about 10 minutes. Remove the saucepan from the heat, and add the thyme and the whole egg yolk.

Rub the toast with the remaining garlic clove. Serve the toast with the soup.

Silvio Viglietti
Il Palma di Alassio
Alassio, Imperia, Italy

Zuppa di Pesce I

(Fish Soup)
Yield: 4 servings

Each region of Italy has its own version of fish stew (in French, bouillabaisse), often made with less expensive varieties of fish. Zuppa di Pesce always includes two or more kinds of fish, squid, or shellfish.

2 pounds mixed fish and shellfish: jumbo shrimp (shelled); squid (cleaned and skinned), cuttlefish (cleaned and beaten); mussels (scrubbed and debearded); whiting, redfish, etc. (scaled)
2 tablespoons olive oil
1/2 cup white wine
2 onions, sliced
2 garlic cloves
2 tablespoons chopped fresh parsley
1 tablespoon tomato paste
2 tablespoons white wine vinegar
Salt and pepper to taste

Slice the squid and cuttlefish in rings. Cut the large fish into pieces.

Warm the oil in a heavy saucepan. Add the cuttlefish, if you are using it. Saute for about 10 minutes, depending on the size of the pieces. Then the squid. Add the wine and continue to cook over slow heat. When the squid looks nearly cooked, add the shellfish and other fish and simmer for another 2 minutes.

With a slotted spoon, remove all the fish and shellfish to a serving bowl. To the remaining juices in the pan, add the sliced onions, garlic, and parsley, and let them "sweat" for a few minutes. Then add the tomato paste and 1/4 cup warm water, and simmer for 40 minutes. Return the fish to the pot and add the vinegar. Season with salt and pepper and simmer for 10 minutes. Serve immediately, or cool and refrigerate the soup for reheating later.

Enzo Cortese
Mulino Trattoria
East Sydney, Australia

Zuppa alla Contadina

(Italian Country Soup)
Yield: 4 servings

1/4 cup olive oil
1 small onion, chopped
1 garlic clove, minced
2 celery ribs with leaves, chopped
1 small carrot, chopped
1 potato, peeled and chopped
1 tomato, chopped
2 tablespoons tomato paste
Pinch chopped fresh parsley
1 teaspoon salt
1/2 teaspoon black pepper
1 quart chicken or beef stock
Grated Parmesan cheese
Extra-virgin olive oil

Heat 1/4 cup olive oil in a stockpot. Add the vegetables; stir in the tomato paste, parsley, salt, and pepper. Saute until the vegetables are softened. Add the broth and heat until the soup begins to boil.

Ladle the hot soup into individual bowls. Sprinkle with Parmesan cheese, then olive oil, and serve.

Mario Di Fillippis
Buca Di San Francesco
Arezzo, Italy

Zuppa di Pesce II

(Fish Soup)
Yield: 4 to 6 servings

2 tablespoons olive oil
1/2 medium-size onion, minced
4 shallots, minced
2 to 3 garlic cloves, minced
1/2 teaspoon dried thyme
1/2 teaspoon dried tarragon
1/2 teaspoon dried oregano
1/2 teaspoon crushed hot red pepper
1/2 to 3/4 cup white wine
8 to 10 medium shrimp in their shells
8 to 10 mussels, scrubbed and debearded
About 1/2 pound scallops
8 to 10 clams, scrubbed and rinsed
2 cups fish stock, clam juice, or water
1 pound uncooked pasta (preferably linguine)
Chopped fresh parsley

Optional

Lobster tails, sea bass or monkfish fillet, squid
  (cleaned and skinned), or eels (skinned,
  cleaned, and cut into pieces)
1 tablespoon vegetable oil (if using fish)

In a large, heavy saucepan, heat the olive oil over medium heat. Add the onion, shallots, and garlic and saute until translucent. Add the thyme, tarragon, oregano, and red pepper. Stir; add the white wine. After the wine stops sizzling (a few seconds), add the seafood. (If you are using sea bass or monkfish, lightly flour it and brown it separately in vegetable oil, drain, and add last.) When all the seafood has been added, pour in the fish stock or clam juice (water will do in a pinch, but it will not produce as rich a broth). Cover and simmer over low to medium heat for approximately 15 minutes.

While the seafood simmers, cook the pasta in a large pot of boiling water. Drain and place in a large serving bowl. Pour the seafood over the pasta, and top with plenty of parsley. Serve with sauteed fresh spinach or escarole.

Pietro Mosconi
Villa Mosconi Restaurant
New York, New York

17

Minestra Di Lenticche

(Lentil Soup)
Yield: 4 servings

Lentils are popular throughout Italy. In some areas, they are served on New Year's to bring wealth in the coming year.

The greenish-brown Italian lentils tend to remain whole better than the common variety. If you can find them, use them for this recipe.

1/2 pound (or slightly less) green lentils
1 bay leaf
2 leaves fresh sage or 1/8 teaspoon dried
2 tablespoons oil
3 slices bacon, julienned
1 garlic clove, minced
3 celery ribs, chopped
1 medium-size onion, chopped
2 tablespoons tomato paste
Salt and pepper to taste
1/4 pound uncooked ditalini
Grated Parmesan cheese (optional)

Simmer the lentils in 3 quarts water with the bay leaf and sage. Do not allow the water to boil too rapidly or the lentils will break.

Meanwhile, heat the oil in a large saucepan, add the bacon, and cook until limp. Add the garlic, celery, and onion, and continue to saute slowly. Dilute the tomato paste in 1/2 cup hot water, and add to the saucepan. Add the salt and pepper. Cook for 20 minutes.

When the lentils are tender, add the tomato sauce. Taste for salt, and add water if the soup is too thick. Bring the soup to a boil again; add the pasta. Cook for 10 more minutes. Remove the bay leaf and sage. Serve with grated Parmesan, if desired.

Richard Cicchi
Santa Barbara, California

Zuppa di Fagioli

(Bean Soup)
Yield: 4 servings

Spinach beet (*barbatietola*) is a beet grown for its greens; its root is not eaten. Other greens can be substituted.

1 pound dry small white beans
3 tablespoons olive oil
1 red onion, finely chopped
2 small carrots, finely chopped
2 celery ribs, finely chopped
1 tablespoon tomato puree
1 1/2 pounds Swiss chard, spinach beet, or beet greens, finely chopped
Salt and pepper to taste
1 beef bouillon cube
4 slices hard, stale bread
1/2 red onion or 1 scallion, chopped

Soak the beans overnight in water to cover. Drain and rinse. Place in a pot with plenty of water and simmer until soft, 1 to 2 hours.

Heat the oil in saucepan. Add the onion, carrots, and celery and saute for 10 minutes. Add the tomato puree, the greens, salt and pepper, and bouillon cube; simmer for 15 minutes. Add the beans with the cooking water and simmer for 1 hour, adding more water if the soup gets too thick.

Place the bread in individual bowls. Pour the soup over the bread, and let sit for 5 minutes. Sprinkle the red onion over the soup and serve.

Mary Bailey
Taverna dei Barbi
Montalcino, Siena, Italy

Passato di Patate
con Aglio Arrosto

(Cream of Potato Soup with Roasted Garlic)
Yield: 4 to 6 servings

In the land of pasta and rice, potatoes have never become commonplace as they have in the rest of Europe, even though they have been cultivated in Italy since the late 1500s. Potatoes are found mainly in the North, where they are often made into gnocchi. Here they are combined with roasted garlic to make an exquisite soup with a mellow garlic flavor.

4 whole garlic bulbs
Virgin olive oil
1/4 pound unsalted butter
2 leeks, chopped
10 large new red potatoes, peeled and cut into chunks
2 cups homemade chicken stock
2 cups heavy cream
1 sprig fresh thyme, minced
Salt and pepper to taste

Slice the top off of each head of garlic so that each clove is exposed. Place exposed side up in a shallow baking pan. Drizzle liberally with olive oil. Cover the pan with foil and bake at 275°F for 2 hours.

Place the butter and leeks in a heavy 2-quart saucepan. Saute over low heat for 10 minutes. Add the potatoes and cook, stirring occasionally, for 15 minutes. Add the chicken stock, cover, and simmer until the vegetables are very tender.

Squeeze the roasted garlic cloves into the saucepan. Puree the contents of the pan in a food processor or blender to a very smooth consistency. Return the soup to the pan, and add the cream, thyme, and salt and pepper. Serve hot.

Lucia Demeo
Pastabella
San Francisco, California

Italian Wedding Soup

Yield: 12 servings

Meatballs

1/2 pound lean ground beef
1/4 cup chopped fresh parsley
1 1/2 teaspoons salt
1 1/2 teaspoons black pepper
1/2 cup grated Parmesan cheese
2 eggs

Soup

3 tablespoons clarified butter or olive oil
1 1/2 cups diced onion
1 1/2 cups diced celery
1 1/4 cups diced carrots
1 bunch fresh escarole, chopped
1 small bunch fresh chicory, trimmed
1 bay leaf
Salt and pepper to taste
8 cups chicken broth
1 pound boneless chicken breast
4 ounces uncooked thin egg noodles
1/4 cup grated Parmesan cheese

Combine the meatball ingredients in a bowl; mix them well by hand. Set aside.

Heat the clarified butter in a large soup kettle. Add the vegetables, and saute for 10 to 15 minutes, or until they are half-cooked. Add the bay leaf and salt and pepper. Pour in the chicken broth. Simmer for about 1 hour.

While the soup simmers, steam or bake the chicken meat until done, 35 to 40 minutes. Cool, then slice it into strips. Roll the ground beef mixture into 3/4-inch balls. Add the meatballs and the chicken strips to the soup. Simmer for 10 minutes.

Meanwhile cook the egg noodles according to the package directions. Drain the noodles and add them to the soup. Stir in the remaining 1/4 cup Parmesan cheese and serve.

Joe Yacavone
Pasta Palace in the Palace Station Hotel and Casino
Las Vegas, Nevada

Zuppa di Pesce alla Barese

(Fish Soup, Bari-Style)
Yield: 4 servings

This recipe for fish stew comes from Signora Delia (Lennie) Conenna, a native of Bari, an ancient city on the Southern Adriatic coast. If Paris had the sea, it would be a little Bari, or so say the natives.

4 large thin steaks of dogfish, grouper, or other large fish
1/2 cup olive oil
2 garlic cloves, minced
1 pound, 10 ounces fresh (or 1 1/2 pounds canned) tomatoes, peeled and roughly chopped
2 tablespoons chopped fresh parsley
Salt and pepper to taste
5 to 7 ounces black olives (preferably small ones)

Heat the olive oil in a wide, low-sided, flame-proof dish (the Italian dish of this sort is called a *teglia*). Add the garlic and saute for a few minutes. As soon as the oil begins to "sing," add the tomatoes, the parsley, and salt and pepper. Cook for a few minutes over medium heat; then add the olives. Add the fish steaks and cook until they turn fully white, no longer, 5 to 10 minutes. Serve hot.

Delia Conenna
La Buca
Bari, Italy

Pasta
&
Sauces

The book *De Onesta Voluptate*, written in the Middle Ages, honors Signor Meluzza of Como (near Milan) as the inventor of spaghetti (he prepared his with oil and garlic). The *Onesta Voluptate* is on display at the Museum of Pasta in Pontedassio, on the Ligurian Sea, along with other books and drawings that "prove" that pasta originated in northern Italy.

Actually the debate still rages over whether the Italians or the Chinese invented pasta. My opinion is that while China long ago introduced rice-flour noodles, the Italians were first to make semolina wheat pasta—which is what we traditionally think of as pasta, despite the currently fashionable trend of calling any noodle dish pasta, no matter what its ingredients or country of origin. Actually, the ancient Greeks and the Etruscans both left evidence that they made some sort of noodle, well before the Romans. In any event, by the time of the Renaissance, pasta was widely known, though it remained a luxury food enjoyed by the wealthy and served by the common folk only on special occasions.

Pasta did not become a daily dish in Italy until someone thought of flavoring it with tomatoes, a vegetable native to the Americas. A strain of yellow tomatoes reached Italy in the sixteenth century, but it wasn't until two Jesuit priests brought over from Mexico some seed of the red variety that tomatoes gained a foothold in the cuisine. Of all the Europeans, the Neapolitans were the most enthusiastic about the tomato—and about pasta.

By 1700 some 60 shops were selling pasta in Naples. Some 80 years later, there were almost 300, and pasta was firmly established. Today, pasta is a regular part of the Italian menu. It is usually served as a first course, although a typical meal of country people of the South is a pasta dish, followed by a salad. At lunch, a modest dish of pasta serves as the main course, followed by cheese and fruit.

Pasta was first introduced into the United States by Thomas Jefferson in 1786, when he returned from his travels as ambassador to France. The first commercial pasta plant appeared near the Brooklyn Bridge in New York in 1848, but it wasn't until the great waves of Italian immigration at the turn of the century that pasta finally caught on in America.

The generic term *pasta* includes a multitude of products made from semolina or flour and water or eggs, then dried in various shapes and forms, each one of which has its own, usually very descriptive, name. Each region of Italy has a specially shaped pasta, the variations limited only by the imagination. Italian grocery stores carry all types of dried pasta, *pasta secca*. There is often *pasta fresca*, fresh pasta, for sale as well.

It's a tempting adventure to make your own *pasta fresca* (fresh, or homemade, pasta). It's not at all difficult to make, and it can be made speedily with the help of a food processor and pasta roller.

Keep in mind that fresh is not necessarily better than dried when it comes to pasta, particularly when you are comparing high-quality Italian imports to fresh supermarket brands. Taste and compare yourself. Furthermore, fresh pasta comes in a limited number of shapes. When a recipe calls for a particular pasta, it is the one best suited for the recipe. In general, long, thin pasta, such as spaghetti, is best suited for light sauces based on olive oil. Thicker long shapes, such as fettuccine, are best with heavier cream, meat, and cheese sauces. Sauces made with vegetables or beans should be matched with medium-size tubular pastas. Rigatoni and penne are traditionally baked. The following glossary only touches on the innumerable shapes of pasta. Many of the descriptions mention size as well as use, but you can often judge the size from the Italian suffix. "Oni" means large. "Elle," "ina," and "ti" are all diminutives, meaning the pasta is small.

When cooking pasta, follow the directions on the package and helpful hints listed under "Pasta Pointers" later in this chapter. Remember that, regardless of cooking time indicated, all pasta is done when it is *al dente* (literally, "by the tooth") —when a bite tells you it is firm but tender.

Pasta Shapes

These shapes are all available in the U.S. Most can be found in Italian markets and specialty food stores, if not at your supermarket.

Agnolatti. "Fat little lambs." Plump, semi-circular or square ravioli filled with meat. A holiday favorite of the Piedmont region.

Alphabets. Tiny pasta letters.

Angel Hair (*Capelli d'Angeli*). Fine, long, coiled strands of pasta called angel hair because of the fineness, used in soups or with sauces.

Anelli. "Little rings" for soup.

Anellini. Tinier rings.

Anolini. Round or ring-shaped ravioli, served with sauce or in a broth.

Ave Maria. So named because they are shaped like rosary beads. Short tubular pasta for soup.

Bacatilli (or *Perclateli*). Thin spaghetti with a hole through the middle, used like spaghetti.

Bows (or *Farfalle*). "Butterflies" come in small, medium, and large and in colored vegetable flavors. They can be made with eggs or just flour and water.

Cannelloni. A large (usually 4-inch to 6-inch) tubular pasta that can be stuffed with a number of fillings: spinach, ricotta, meat, or a combination. "Large reeds" is the translation. They can be made fresh or are available in dried squares or tubes.

Capellini (or *Fideo, Fidelini*). "Fine hairs" to be used in soup or with sauce, often sold coiled; they are not as fine as angel hair.

Capelleti. "Little hats" can be made with fresh dough and stuffed or bought dried and used like macaroni.

Cavatelli. A short, curled noodle formed like a shell.

Conchiglie, Conchigliette (or *Maruzze, Maruzelle*). "Conch shells" come in a variety of sizes from tiny shells for soup to giant shells for stuffing. They can be either smooth or ridged.

Creste di Galli. "Cockscombs" can be used in place of medium-size elbow macaroni.

Ditali, Ditalini (or *Tubbetti*). "Thimbles" of macaroni cut in short lengths, about 1/4 inch in diameter by 1/2 inch long. Used in soups.

Ditali Rigati. "Ridged thimbles"; they can be sauced, baked, or used in salads.

Elbow Macaroni. Short, curved tubes of pasta, available in many vegetable colors and sizes, from tiny elbows for soups to 1-inch elbows for casseroles.

Farfalle, Farfallette, Farfalloni (see *Bows*).

Fettuccine, Fettuccelle. "Little ribbons." A long, flat noodle, about 1/4-inch to 3/8-inch wide. Fettuccine is the Roman version of tagliatelle, most commonly found in yellow or green. Often made fresh, but also available dried, straight or in coils. Fettuccine combines well with most sauces.

Fideo, Fidelini (see *Capellini*).

Fusilli. Long strands of pasta twisted like a corkscrew and used in place of spaghetti. Some manufacturers use the name fusilli for rotelle.

Funghini. Intricate, baby-size "mushrooms" for soup.

Garganelli. Ridged, rolled tubes with diagonal-cut ends. Used in baked pasta dishes.

Gemelli. "Twins." Paired strands of spaghetti about 3 inches long, twisted like embroidery thread. Used like spaghetti.

Gnocchi. Homemade "lumps" that look like dumplings. They can be made with mashed potatoes, cornmeal, ricotta cheese, or semolina. Manufacturers make a dried gnocchi to be used as one would use medium-size elbow macaroni.

Lasagna, Lasagne. Flat, wide sheets of pasta, with straight or curly edges on one or both sides, in yellow or green, for a baked layered meat and cheese dish. Size varies from 1 to 2-1/2 inches wide.

Linguine, Linguini. "Little tongues" are long, thin, flat noodles, halfway between a flat ribbon and a cylindrical strand. Linguine is thinner than fettuccine, wider than spaghetti.

Lumache. "Snails" come in small and medium sizes for salads, baked dishes, and sauced entrées. Use as you would use medium elbows.

Macaroni. This is the U.S. pasta industry's generic term for any dried wheat pasta product. More commonly, macaroni means dried pasta tubes.

Maccheroni (*Macaroni*). Hollow pasta. Elbow macaroni has a slight bend in the middle. Other shapes include bucatini, cannolichi, and ziti.

Maccheroni alla Chitarra. Noodles made on a noodle-cutting instrument that is strung with wires like a guitar, producing long, hollow macaroni.

Mafalde, Mafaldine. Long noodles, about 3/4 inch wide, rippled on both edges (the thinner version being mafaldine). Sauce as for spaghetti or fettuccine.

Maltagliati. Hard-to-find flat noodles with diagonal-cut or pointed ends. Use as you would egg noodles, fettuccine.

Manicotti. "Little muffs" are actually one of the larger tubes of pasta available, ribbed or smooth, for stuffing, saucing, and baking.

Margherita. "Daisy" noodles don't look like daisies. They are about as wide as fettuccine and have one curly edge.

Maruzzel, Maruzze, Maruzelle. A variety of "conch shell" (*conchiglie*) for soups (tiny shells) or stuffing (large shells).

Monti. American ravioli resembling little boats.

Mostaccoli (or *Penne*). "Mustaches" are 2-inch-long, smooth or ridged, diagonal-cut tubes resembling quill pens (*penne*). They are good with a chunky meat sauce or robust tomato sauce.

Occhi di Lupo. "Wolf's eyes" are thick, elbow-like tubes, 1 1/2 inches long. Good with robust sauces.

Occhi di Pernice. Little "partridge eyes" for soup.

Orzo. "Barley" for soup, sometimes cooked like rice.

Pansotti. "Potbellied" triangular ravioli. These are popular around Genoa.

Pappardelle. A thin, lasagne-like noodle, 1 inch wide, often homemade with pinked edges. These are served with rabbit in Tuscany.

Pastina. General term used for tiny pasta meant for soup.

Paternoster Rigati. "Our Father" pasta is named after beads of the rosary; they are small ridged pastina for soup.

Penne, Pennette (see *Mostaccoli*). Diagonal-cut, plain or ribbed.

Perciatelle, Bucatini. Flat, hollow spaghetti.

Ravioli. Usually square pasta stuffed with eggs, vegetables, meat, or cheese and served with sauce or in soup. Other (smaller) ravioli are called anolotti or raviolini.

Ricci, Riccini. "Little curls" about 1 1/2 inches long. Use as you would use medium-size macaroni.

Rigatoni. Large ribbed tubes, good with chunky sauces. About 1 1/2 to 3 inches long.

Rotelle. "Little wheels" that are actually corkscrew or spiral shaped. Sometimes also called fusilli, but wider than fusilli. Use as you would medium-size macaroni.

Ruote. "Wheels" that look like their name. Use as you would medium-sized macaroni.

Semi di Melone. "Melon seeds" pastina.

Spaghetti, Spaghettini, Spaghettoni. "Little strands" are the best-known pasta and can be thick or thin. Other varieties of spaghetti are capellini, fidelini, vermicelli.

Stuffed Pasta (*Ravioli, Cappelleti, Tortellini*). The stuffing can be fish, chicken, meat, cheese, vegetables, or a combination. They are served with sauce or melted butter.

Tagliatelle, Tagliolette, Tagliolini, Tagliarini. The verb *tagliare* means "to cut" and these are narrow-cut egg noodles, 1/8-inch to 3/4-inch wide. Similar to fettuccine in appearance and use, these are the Bolognese version of fettuccine.

Tonnarelli. Square-cut spaghetti.

Tortiglioni. Wider than rotelle corkscrew but similar in appearance and use.

Tortellini (see also *Capelletti*). "Little twists" rumored to have been modeled after Venus's navel. A Bolognese specialty, filled like ravioli and served with sauce or in soup. Tortellini have smooth edges rather than ruffled ones as capelletti.

Tripolini. Named to honor Italy's conquest of Tripoli, these 1/2-inch crimped-in-the-middle pastas go in soups or salads or can be served with a simple sauce.

Tufoli (see *Rigatoni*).

Vermicelli. "Little worms." Thicker than angel hair, thinner than spaghetti, sold either in straight rods, or in a bow-knot of 15 or 20 strands, or coiled.

Wheels (see *Ruote*).

Ziti. "Bridegrooms" are tubular macaroni, sometimes sold long, then broken into pieces for cooking. They are thinner than mostaccoli but used similarly.

Pasta Pointers

If you are not going to serve it right away, fresh pasta can be stored in the refrigerator for about a week or in the freezer for 2 to 3 months. Uncooked dry pasta can be stored for up to 1 year in a cool, dry place.

Most dry pasta doubles in volume when cooked, so when measuring uncooked portions, half of what would seem a single serving is a full serving. Measure uncooked dry pasta by weight rather than volume for recipe accuracy. Generally, a serving of pasta is about 2 ounces of cooked or fresh pasta for a first course or side dish; 3 to 4 ounces for the main course.

Use a large, deep pot and about 4 quarts of water for each pound of pasta (1 quart for every 4 ounces, or 2 main course servings). Bring the water to a rapid boil before adding the pasta for even cooking without sticking. Lasagna noodles may require a tablespoon or two of oil in the water to prevent sticking or tearing.

If the pasta is to be used in a casserole, reduce the boiling time by about one-third. The pasta will soften as the casserole bakes.

Pasta is at its best freshly cooked and hot, but it can be kept fresh in the refrigerator for up to 1 week if it is tossed with a bit of butter to prevent sticking. To reheat, drop into boiling water briefly, drain, and use immediately. A tomato-meat sauce often tastes even better after it has been stored in the refrigerator for a few days. If the sauce is mixed with pasta before refrigerating, replace lost moisture with some water before reheating.

The Sauces of Italy

In Italy the sauce is part of the dish, a necessary ingredient. It is used sparingly, not to mask the food, but rather to enhance it. There is a great variety of Italian sauces, and tomato sauce is only one of the many sauces for pasta, meat, fish, poultry, and vegetables.

Aglio-Olio-Peperoncino—Garlic, olive oil, sweet peppers, anchovies, Parmesan

Agra Dolce—Sweet and sour sauce (from Milan)

al Burro—With butter and grated Parmesan

al Peperoncino—Red pepper sauce

al Sugo—With tomato sauce and grated Parmesan

Amatriciana—Tomatoes, red peppers, bacon, onions, garlic

Besciamella—Cream sauce (northern Italy)

Bolognese—Tomatoes, meat, onions, herbs (Bologna)

Carbonara—Smoked ham (bacon), cheese, eggs, olive oil

Carrettiera—Tuna, mushrooms, tomato puree, ground pepper

con le Vongole—Clams, garlic, parsley, pepper, olive oil, sometimes tomatoes

di Fegatini—Chicken liver sauce (over gnocchi)

di Formaggio—Cheese sauce

di Funghi—Mushroom sauce (from Verona)

di Noci—Walnut sauce from northern Italy (over ravioli, fish)

di Pomodoro—Tomato sauce

di Zucchini—Zucchini sauce (from Marches)

Grano en Indiano—Curried corn sauce (Rome)

Marinara—Tomatoes, olives, garlic

Pizzaiola—Thick, unsieved tomato sauce with garlic

Pesto—Basil leaves, garlic, cheese, sometimes pine nuts and marjoram (from Genoa)

Pommarola—Tomatoes, garlic, basil

Puttanesca—Capers, black olives, parsley, garlic, olive oil, black pepper

Ragu—Same as Bolognese

Verde—Parsley, basil, pine nuts

Pasta all'Uovo

(Egg Pasta)
Yield: 3 to 4 servings (about 1 pound)

Many of the restaurants I visited made their own pasta and included a recipe for making pasta along with the sauce recipes I collected. The recipes all call for flour, eggs, and salt. The exact proportions of these ingredients vary significantly, but that has more to do with the type and freshness of flour, the prevailing climate, and the size of the eggs than anything else. The very general rule of thumb is to use 1 medium-size egg to 3/4 cup flour.

What follows is a recipe for making Pasta All'uovo (egg pasta) that works whether you make it the traditional Italian way, mixing the ingredients by hand, or whether you use a food processor.

2 1/4 cups all-purpose unbleached flour
3 eggs
1/4 teaspoon salt

Pour the flour onto a smooth working surface and gather it into a mound. Make a well in the center.

Beat the eggs with the salt and pour into the center of the flour. Start beating the eggs with a fork. With your free hand, push the flour up around the eggs to keep the eggs from spilling onto the table. When the dough can no longer be worked with a fork, knead in the remaining flour with your hands. Continue to knead the dough until it is smooth and elastic and all the flour is worked in. If the dough feels too sticky, add 1 tablespoon of flour at a time and knead it in. If the dough is too dry, add a little beaten egg or oil, a drop at a time.

It helps to allow the dough to rest for about 30 minutes before rolling it out, but is not necessary.

To make the dough in a food processor, place the flour in the bowl of the machine. Mix in the salt. With the motor running, add the eggs, one at a time. Process until the dough forms into a ball. If the dough seems too sticky, add 1 tablespoon of flour and process for an additional minute. Allow the dough to rest for about 15 minutes before rolling.

To roll by hand, divide the dough into 4 pieces. Wrap 3 of the pieces in plastic film to keep them moist. Lightly flour the working surface and rolling pin. Flatten the dough into a pancake. Begin to roll from the center out, until you have a sheet of dough the desired thickness, 1/8 inch to 1/16 inch thick (the thickness of a dime). Let the dough rest for about 15 minutes before cutting into the desired shape.

To use a pasta roller, divide the dough into 4 pieces. Flatten each piece into a pancake and lightly flour. Wrap 3 of the pieces in plastic film to keep them moist. Set the roller on its widest setting and pull the piece of flattened dough through. Run the dough through the roller again and again, reducing the space between the rollers until the pasta has reached the desired thickness. Let the dough rest for about 15 minutes before cutting into the desired shape.

Tagliatelle con Pesto

Yield: 4 servings

Pesto is a Ligurian specialty. The Genoese serve it with pasta, minestrone, or as a flavoring in vegetable dishes. Traditionally, pesto is made with a mortar and pestle (hence the name), but you can use a food processor or blender if you prefer. Well sealed in a jar with a thin film of olive oil sealing out air, pesto can be kept for a week or so in the refrigerator. It also freezes well.

Pesto

1/4 cup basil leaves
1 to 2 garlic cloves
2 to 3 tablespoons pine nuts
Pinch salt
1/4 pound Parmesan cheese, grated (1 cup)
1/4 cup olive oil

Pasta

1 pound tagliatelle or spaghetti

Pound the basil in a mortar with the garlic, pine nuts, and salt. Add the cheese and continue to pound until the mixture is reduced to a paste. Incorporate the oil, little by little, until all has been absorbed.

Cook the pasta in plenty of boiling water, drain. Put the pasta on a heated serving dish or on individual plates. Pour the pesto over the pasta and serve.

Carol Anderson
Castel Doria
Dolceacqua, Imperia, Italy

Tagliatelle al Tartufo

(Noodles with Truffle Sauce)
Yield: 4 servings

Both white and black truffles are found in Italy, but while the black truffle is most prized in French cuisine, the white truffle, which can be eaten uncooked, is more prized in Italian cooking. The flavor and aroma of truffles are almost beyond words. Some describe the white truffle's piquant, earthy flavor as a cross between a clove of garlic and a piece of Parmesan. A little shaving of truffle elevates this simple dish of buttered noodles to heavenly fare.

6 tablespoons butter
1/4 cup olive oil
1 tablespoon chopped onions
1 small truffle (black or white), grated
1 tablespoon chopped fresh parsley
Salt to taste
10 ounces tagliatelle

In a pan, heat the butter and olive oil together. Add the onions and saute briefly. Add the grated truffle, parsley, and salt; saute for a few minutes.

In the meantime, cook the noodles in plenty of boiling salted water until they are almost, but not quite, tender. Drain the noodles, and add them to the pan with the truffle sauce. Mix the pasta and sauce as they cook for a few minutes. Serve immediately.

Alviero Bernardini
al San Francesco
Orvieto, Italy

Alfred's Fettuccine Alfredo

Yield: 4 servings

In Italy, you are likely to encounter this very simple dish as *Fettuccine al burro e Parmigiano*, pasta with butter and Parmesan cheese. With cream added it becomes fettuccine alla panna, noodles with cream sauce. In the *Classic Italian Cookbook*, Marcella Hazan says Alfredo had a restaurant in Rome, where this dish became famous. She reports he used a gold fork and spoon to give each serving of fettuccine a final toss.

1 pound fettuccine
1 pound unsalted butter at room temperature, sliced 1/4 inch thick
1 pound Parmesan cheese, finely grated
Freshly ground black pepper
Minced fresh parsley to taste

Cook the pasta in plenty of boiling water until it is tender but firm. Drain and quickly return the fettuccine to the kettle. Add the butter and cheese, and toss lightly but rapidly until the noodles are evenly coated. Divide the pasta among 4 heated plates. Top with black pepper and parsley.

Variation

Creamed Noodles Alfredo. Toss hot, drained fettuccine with 1 cup melted butter, 2 cups finely grated Parmesan cheese, and 1 cup warm heavy cream. Top with freshly ground black pepper.

Alfred Carangelo
Santa Barbara, California

Fettuccine Napoli

Yield: 4 servings

1 pound sausage meat
1 pound fettuccine
1 teaspoon butter
1/2 teaspoon minced garlic
5 ounces fresh broccoli, chopped
1/2 pound fresh mushrooms, sliced
1/4 teaspoon white pepper
1/4 teaspoon nutmeg
1/2 teaspoon salt
1 1/2 cups half-and-half cream
1 1/2 cups sour cream
1 1/2 cups freshly grated Parmesan cheese

In a large frying pan, brown the sausage meat over medium heat. Drain well on paper towels and crumble. Set aside.

Cook the fettuccine in plenty of boiling water until tender but still firm. Drain.

While the pasta cooks, saute the butter and garlic together in a large saute pan over medium-high heat. Add the broccoli and saute for 3 minutes. Add the mushrooms and crumbled sausage. Add the pepper, nutmeg, and salt, and heat until the sausage is warm. Reduce the heat and slowly stir in the half-and-half and sour cream. Add the Parmesan cheese; heat and stir well. When the cheese has melted and the white sauce is well combined, add the fettuccine. Mix thoroughly. Serve very hot.

Elsie McFarland
Caro Amico
Portland, Oregon

Fettuccine alla Margarita

Yield: 2 servings

This dish, which hails from an Italian restaurant in Ireland, was named for the owner's wife.

24 large mussels, scrubbed and debearded
10 spears broccoli
1/2 pound uncooked fettuccine
2 tablespoons garlic butter
Salt to taste
1 pinch ground cinnamon
1 cup heavy cream
2 tablespoons grated Parmesan cheese
1 teaspoon chopped parsley

Steam the mussels until most of the shells open. Drain and shell the mussels; discard any that have not opened.

At the same time, steam the broccoli until just tender; drain.

While the mussels and broccoli cook, boil the fettuccine in plenty of salted water until tender but still firm. Drain. Melt the garlic butter in a frying pan. Add the salt, cinnamon, and 3/4 cup of the cream, and mix thoroughly.

Divide the pasta between 2 plates. Pour the rest of the cream over the pasta, and sprinkle Parmesan cheese and parsley on top. Toss well. Add the mussels and broccoli and toss again. Spoon the cream sauce over all and serve.

Alberto and Margarita Del Rio
La Taverna
Galway, Republic of Ireland

Fettuccine alla Salvia con Funghi Selvatigo

(Pasta with sage, wild mushrooms, cream, and walnuts)

Yield: 2 to 4 servings

4 tablespoons (unsalted) butter
1 cup heavy cream
1 teaspoon minced garlic
1/4 cup strong chicken stock
Salt and pepper to taste
1 tablespoon olive oil
1/2 pound wild mushrooms (chanterelle, shitaki, oyster, cremini, etc.)
1 tablespoon chopped shallots
1 sprig fresh sage, chopped
1/2 pound fresh fettuccine
Toasted walnut bits

Melt the butter in a medium-size saucepan and set aside.

In a separate saucepan, heat the cream, garlic, and chicken stock; simmer until the liquid is reduced by half. Swirl in the melted butter and season with salt and pepper. Set aside.

In the saucepan in which you melted the butter, heat the olive oil. Add the mushrooms and shallots and saute for 5 minutes. Add the cream sauce and the sage and continue cooking for 2 to 3 minutes.

While the sauce cooks, cook the pasta in plenty of boiling water until tender but still firm. Drain. Toss the pasta with the sauce, and adjust the seasonings if necessary. Serve topped with toasted walnuts.

Helen Sullivan
Avanzare
Chicago, Illinois

Penne al Peperoni

(Penne with Peppers)
Yield: 6 servings

While traveling in Florence, I made the acquaintance of Masha Innocenti, a teacher of Italian cuisine, who shared with me this recipe. It's a first course of short pasta seasoned with a 3-colored pepper puree and cream. The dish is very popular with the students at Mrs. Innocenti's cooking school.

Sauce

1/2 cup olive oil
1 medium-size green bell pepper, julienned
1 medium-size red bell pepper, julienned
2 medium-size yellow bell peppers, julienned
1 teaspoon salt
1/2 red onion, finely chopped
2/3 cup light cream
1/2 teaspoon dried oregano
5 tablespoons finely chopped fresh parsley
Freshly ground black pepper

Pasta

1 pound, 5 ounces penne or ridged mostaccoli
3 tablespoons salt

Heat the olive oil in a large frying pan over a medium to low flame. Add the peppers, along with the salt and onion, and gently saute until the peppers are tender, 15 to 20 minutes. With a slotted spoon to drain off excess oil, place the peppers and onion in a blender or food processor, add the cream, and blend on high speed until the sauce is completely smooth. Set aside.

To cook the pasta, add the 3 tablespoons salt to 7 to 8 quarts of water and bring to a boil in a very large (10 quart) covered pot. Add the pasta, separating the pieces immediately with a wooden spoon.

While the pasta is boiling, drain the frying pan of oil and reheat the cream sauce in it. Add the oregano and chopped parsley.

When the pasta is done, drain it, reserving at least 1/2 cup of the cooking water. Place the pasta in a serving bowl, add the sauce and the cooking water, and toss gently to mix thoroughly. Serve the pasta hot, sprinkled with freshly ground black pepper.

Masha Innocenti
Italian Cuisine in Cooking School
Florence, Italy

Maria's Pasta Primavera

(Pasta with Spring Vegetables)
Yield: 4 servings

1 pound pasta (mostaccoli or rigatoni)
1 tablespoon olive oil
2 garlic cloves, minced
4 cups diced zucchini
1 cup chicken broth
2 cups sliced fresh mushrooms
1 cup fresh basil leaves
2 cups chopped broccoli
2 tomatoes, diced

While the pasta is cooking, heat the olive oil in a large saucepan. Add the garlic and saute until golden brown, then add the zucchini and chicken broth. Cook the zucchini briefly, until it is tender but still crisp. Add the mushrooms, basil, and broccoli. Cook until all vegetables are done.

When the pasta is tender, but firm, drain and place the pasta in a large serving bowl or on individual plates. Add the vegetables, and toss gently. Garnish with the diced tomatoes and serve.

Maria Perri
The Bootlegger
Las Vegas, Nevada

Spaghetti alla Carbonara

(Spaghetti, Charcoal Maker's Style)
Yield: 1 serving

This is a very popular pasta dish that originated in Rome. Its popularity was spread outside of Italy by Allied soldiers, who perhaps appreciated the dish for its familiar ingredients: the bacon, cheese, and eggs.

The white wine here is used by the chef to cut the fattiness of the bacon.

2 tablespoons oil
2 slices bacon, cut into bite-size pieces
1/2 tablespoon white wine
3 ounces spaghetti
1 egg, lightly beaten
Grated Parmesan cheese

Heat the oil in a frying pan. Add the bacon and wine and fry until the bacon is crisp. With a slotted spoon remove the bacon pieces to paper towels and reserve the drippings.

Cook the spaghetti in plenty of boiling salted water until *al dente*. Drain the spaghetti, return it to the empty pot, and immediately add the bacon drippings and raw egg. (The spaghetti must be very hot when the egg is poured over it so the egg will cook a bit. Toss for a couple of minutes until the egg begins to thicken. Drain slightly, place the pasta in a serving bowl, and sprinkle with the bacon pieces and Parmesan cheese.

Salvatore Guida
Osteria Da Salvatore
Rome, Italy

Salsa alla Don Abbondio

Yield: 2 servings

This is a typical meat and cheese sauce from Calabria, the toe of the Italian boot.

1/4 cup butter
1 garlic clove, minced
1/2 pound ground veal
1/4 cup white wine
1 cup heavy cream
1/4 pound Gorgonzola cheese
1/4 teaspoon dried oregano
1/4 teaspoon black pepper
3 ounces Romano cheese, grated
1/2 pound rigatoni
Chopped fresh parsley

In a large saute pan over high heat, melt the butter. Add the garlic and saute until golden. Add the ground veal and saute until the liquid from the veal is reduced. Add the wine and heavy cream. Bring to a boil and reduce the liquid by half. Add Gorgonzola cheese, oregano, and pepper. Cover and simmer briefly. Add the Romano cheese.

Cook the pasta in plenty of boiling salted water. Drain and pour onto a serving platter. Pour the sauce over the top with a sprinkling of parsley for color.

Michele Riccio
Rudy's Ristorante Italiano & Pizzeria
Seattle, Washington

Boccalino's Linguine Gorgonzola

Yield: 1 serving

1 tablespoon olive oil
1/4 pound boneless breast of chicken, cut in strips
6 julienned slices sweet red pepper
1/3 cup crumbled Gorgonzola cheese
6 tablespoons chicken stock
White pepper to taste
1/4 cup heavy cream
7 broccoli florets, blanched
1/4 pound fresh linguine

Heat the olive oil in a frying pan. Add the chicken and the red peppers, and saute them until they are cooked half through. Add the Gorgonzola, chicken stock, white pepper, and cream. Cook until the liquid is reduced by half.

While the sauce cooks, boil the linguine in plenty of boiling salted water until tender, but firm. Drain. To serve, add the blanched broccoli and cooked linguine to the sauce; toss and serve.

Thea Fink
Ristorante Boccalino
Denver, Colorado

Conchiglioni al Peperoni

(Shell Pasta with Peppers)
Yield: 4 servings

1 pound conchiglioni
2 green peppers
6 tablespoons olive oil
1 1/2 pounds tomatoes, diced
1 garlic clove
1 cup minced fresh parsley
2 tablespoons grated Romano cheese
Salt and pepper to taste

Cook the pasta in plenty of boiling salted water for about 5 minutes. Drain and set aside.

Blanch the peppers in boiling water to cover for 2 minutes. Rinse under cold water. Core and seed them; then cut into strips.

Heat the olive oil in a large saute pan. Saute the pepper strips in the hot olive oil until tender, about 3 minutes. Remove them with a slotted spoon, and set aside. Add the tomatoes to the oil with the garlic and parsley. Simmer for 5 minutes; then add the peppers. Stir in the pasta and mix it with the sauce. Stir in the grated cheese, season with salt and pepper, and serve at once.

Giancarlo Baroncini
Cavalieri Hilton International Roma
Rome, Italy

Chicken Tetrazzini

Yield: 6 servings

People have eaten an unfortunate number of tetrazzini dishes, made from leftovers and served as school lunches and with other institutional fare, but the original dish is quite tasty. According to legend, this famous pasta dish was named for the Italian coloratura soprano Luisa Tetrazzini, and it is worthy of an aria.

Chicken and Stock

5-pound to 6-pound stewing hen, with giblets
1 1/2 teaspoons salt
1 small yellow onion
1 medium-size carrot
1 celery stalk
1 bay leaf
3 to 4 peppercorns
1 pound spaghettini or linguine

Sauce

1/2 cup butter or margarine
1/2 pound mushrooms, sliced
1/4 cup flour, sifted
2 cups reserved chicken stock
1 1/2 cups milk, or 3/4 cup each milk and dry white wine
1 cup heavy cream
2 teaspoons salt
1/8 teaspoon white pepper
1 to 2 tablespoons lemon juice (optional)
1/8 teaspoon nutmeg (optional)

Topping

3/4 cup finely ground fresh bread crumbs
3/4 cup grated Parmesan cheese

Remove the fat from the body cavity of the hen. Then combine the hen, giblets, salt, onion, carrot, celery, bay leaf, and peppercorns with 1 quart of water in a large heavy kettle. Cover, bring to a boil, and reduce to a simmer. Remove the chicken liver after 10 to 15 minutes; cool and reserve it. Simmer the hen for a total of about 2 hours, until tender. Cool the hen in the stock, then skin the meat and remove the bones. Cut the meat into bite-size chunks and dice all the giblets, including the liver. Skim the stock of fat, strain, and reserve it.

Preheat the oven to 350°F.

Cook the pasta in plenty of boiling water until tender but still firm.

While the pasta is cooking, make the sauce. Melt 1/4 cup of the butter in a heavy pan over moderate heat. Add the mushrooms and saute until limp. Add the remaining 1/4 cup butter and heat until melted. Blend in the flour. Add 2 cups chicken stock and the remaining sauce ingredients and heat, stirring, until thickened. Remove from the heat and keep warm.

When the pasta is cooked al dente, drain it and combine it with the sauce and chicken. Place in a buttered, shallow, 3-quart casserole. Mix together the bread crumbs and Parmesan cheese, and sprinkle the topping over the chicken and pasta.

Bake, uncovered, for 30 to 40 minutes, until bubbly. Brown quickly under a broiler and serve.

Ron Frieborn
Indian Wells, California

Pappardelle all'Ortolana

(Pappardelle Farmer's Style)
Yield: 4 servings

This dish is a house specialty of Piccola Roma, a wonderful Roman restaurant where you can sample all the Roman specialties. It's located in the historical center near Palazzo Montecitorio, the seat of the Italian Parliament.

Pappardelle is a type of homemade noodles. They are usually about 3/4 inch wide and cut with a fluted pastry wheel.

6 artichokes, cleaned
About 2 tablespoons olive oil
2 cups fresh asparagus tips
2 cups sliced fresh mushrooms
1 cup fresh peas
1/2 onion
1 pound pasta, preferably papparadelle or
   fettuccine
1/2 pint light or heavy cream
2 tablespoons butter
4 ounces cooked ham, cut into cubes
Grated Parmesan cheese

Place the artichokes in a deep pan with about 1 1/2 inches of water and a bit of olive oil; cover and simmer for about 30 minutes, or until the artichokes are tender (check with a fork). Cut the artichokes into small pieces, and set them aside.

While the artichokes cook, prepare the other vegetables. Boil the asparagus tips in salted water for 15 minutes; drain, and set aside. Heat 1 tablespoon of the olive oil in a skillet, add the mushrooms, and saute for 10 minutes (add a bit more oil if the mushrooms begin to stick); set the mushrooms aside.

Boil the peas in salted water with half an onion, uncut, and a bit of olive oil. Discard the onion and reserve the drained peas.

Cook the pasta in plenty of boiling water until tender but still firm. Drain.

While the pasta is cooking, make the sauce. In a large skillet, heat the cream and butter. When the butter is melted, add the ham. Heat briefly and then add all the vegetables. Heat for about 5 minutes, stirring occasionally, until all the ingredients are heated through.

Toss the pasta into the skillet with the sauce. If the noodles stick together, pour in a little more cream. Add a bit of grated Parmesan cheese. Toss until the vegetables are uniformly distributed, and serve hot.

Roberto Gentile
Piccolo Roma
Rome, Italy

Tagliatelle al Cucciolo

Yield: 10 servings

Naples is known for its pizza, but that doesn't mean other wonderful dishes can't be had there. This original pasta dish, rich with butter, bacon, cheese, and fresh vegetables, is served at a restaurant by the name of al Cucciolo, "the puppy." Why this name was chosen I couldn't say.

1 tablespoon olive oil
3 cups chopped onions
2/3 pound pancetta, cut into strips
1 pound vine-ripened tomatoes, chopped
1 cup fresh or frozen peas
2 cups hot chicken stock
2 pounds tagliatelle
2/3 pound Parmesan cheese, grated
1/2 pound (2 sticks) butter, cut into small pieces
5 egg yolks
Pinch nutmeg
2 cups cream
1/2 pound mozzarella cheese, sliced

In a large ovenproof pan, heat the olive oil. Add the onions and saute until the onions are browned, 10 to 15 minutes. Add the pancetta and the tomatoes; saute for 10 minutes. Then add the peas and the chicken stock and simmer gently.

Cook the tagliatelle in boiling salted water until tender but still firm. When done, fold the noodles into the sauce and sprinkle with the Parmesan cheese. Mix well, then fold in the butter.

Beat the egg yolks with the nutmeg and cream. Fold this mixture into the tagliatelle. Lay the mozzarella slices over the noodles. Bake in a 450°F oven about 10 minutes. Serve hot.

Carmine Esposito Alaia
Ristorante al Cucciolo
Naples, Italy

Chocolate Fettuccine with Caviar

Yield: 4 servings

This elegant first course from Laurenzo's Gourmet Italian Restaurant won an award for "The Best Pasta in the City of Miami, 1986" from the National Pasta Association. Chocolate fettuccine is made by tinting pasta dough with cocoa. If chocolate fettuccine is not available, substitute plain fettuccine. Spanish caviar is the best caviar for this dish as it will retain its shape when cooked.

1 pound chocolate fettuccine
1 teaspoon finely chopped shallots
1 teaspoon Spanish caviar
1/4 cup heavy cream
1 tablespoon cognac
Pinch black pepper
1 tablespoon grated Parmesan cheese
1 tablespoon butter
1 ounce semi-sweet chocolate, grated

Cook the pasta in plenty of boiling salted water until tender but still firm. Drain.

In a large frying pan over high heat, place the cooked fettuccine. Quickly add all the other ingredients, except the chocolate, mix well, and cook uncovered until the sauce thickens, approximately 10 to 15 minutes. Serve garnished with chocolate.

Chef Emilio
Laurenzo's Gourmet Italian Restaurant
North Miami Beach, Florida

Pennette Arrabbiate

(Angry Pennette)
Yield: 4 servings

The "angry" pasta is hot, pleasantly hot from red chile peppers. This is a quick dish to make; you can prepare the sauce while the pasta is cooking.

4 teaspoons olive oil
2 garlic cloves
1 small dry red chile, finely chopped
1/4 cup finely chopped fresh parsley
3 1/2 cups chopped fresh or canned tomatoes, with juice
Salt and pepper to taste
1 pound pennette rigate (short "ribbed" tubes)

While the water heats for the pasta, heat the olive oil in a large saucepan. Add the garlic and chile and fry gently until the garlic is golden. Add half the parsley, and fry for a few seconds until it is "toasted" but not burnt. Immediately add the tomatoes and salt and pepper. Stirring occasionally, heat the sauce gently until the pasta is ready.

In the meantime, cook the pasta in plenty of boiling salted water for 8 to 10 minutes, until not quite tender. Drain the pasta well, and add it to the sauce in the pan. Over low heat, mix the pasta and sauce until any excess liquid is absorbed. Serve sprinkled with the rest of the fresh parsley.

Giovanni Marrone
Taverna 58
Pescara, Italy

Pasta con l'Aglio

(Pasta with Garlic)
Yield: 2 servings

This great Sicilian country dish combines garlic with fresh tomatoes. It is simple to make and simply delicious!

6 plum tomatoes, peeled and finely crushed
6 garlic cloves
1/2 cup olive oil
1/2 cup grated Romano cheese
Salt and pepper to taste
1/2 pound pasta of your choice
Handful fresh basil leaves

While the water heats for the pasta, mix the tomatoes, garlic, and oil in a bowl. Add the grated cheese, salt and pepper.

Cook the pasta in boiling water until tender but still firm. Drain, and place in a serving dish. Add the (uncooked) sauce to the pasta, toss, and garnish with basil leaves. Serve immediately.

Paul DiAmico
Paul DiAmico's Restaurant
Palm Springs, California

Maccheroni alla Calbrese

(Macaroni, Calabria Style)
Yield: 6 servings

Here's another spicy pasta dish, this one with the added richness of Parma ham. The recipe calls for caciocavallo cheese, a piquant cheese made throughout southern Italy. Its name translates as "horse cheese," because it is hung in pairs astride a pole to age and dry. Substitute Parmesan cheese for caciocavallo.

2 1/2 pounds tomatoes
1/2 cup olive oil
1 garlic clove
Small piece hot red chile, finely chopped
1 onion, finely chopped
1/4 pound prosciutto (Parma ham), finely
   chopped
Salt and pepper to taste
5 cups macaroni
1 cup grated caciocavallo cheese

Dip the tomatoes in hot water; then peel them. Halve the tomatoes and discard the seeds. Chop the tomatoes and set aside.

Heat the oil in a large pan, add the garlic and chile pepper and saute briefly. Discard the garlic as soon as it browns. Add the onion, and cook until translucent. Add the ham and continue to cook for 2 to 3 minutes. Add the tomatoes. Season with salt and pepper, increase the heat, and cook briskly for 30 minutes.

Bring a large kettle of salted water to a boil, and cook the macaroni until tender but firm. Drain the pasta, return it to the kettle, and toss it with a little of the sauce. Spread a layer of macaroni in a hot serving dish, sprinkle with plenty of grated cheese, and spread over about 2 tablespoons sauce. Continue layering the ingredients until they are all used up. Serve very hot.

Salvatore Conti
Conti
Reggio-Calabria, Italy

Stelio's Macaroni

Yield: 6 servings

Here's another version of an "angry" pasta dish, this one from Pisa.

3 pounds tomatoes, peeled
3 tablespoons olive oil
1/2 pound (2 sticks) butter, cut into pieces
Salt and pepper to taste
3 garlic cloves
4 small dry red chiles
1 pound macaroni
Grated Pecorino or other hard cheese

While the water heats for the pasta, combine the tomatoes, 2 tablespoons of the olive oil, the butter, and salt and pepper in a saucepan. Bring to a simmer, stirring occasionally.

Mince the garlic and chiles, then grind them with 1 tablespoon olive oil in a blender or food processor. Add to the sauce.

Cook the macaroni in plenty of boiling water until tender but still firm; drain. Add the pasta to the sauce; heat and mix briefly. Serve with grated cheese.

Berretta Stelio
Trattoria da Stelio
Pisa, Italy

Spaghetti, Sicilian Style

Yield: 6 servings

Eggplant and tomatoes are both characteristic of Sicilian cooking.

1 large eggplant
3/4 cup olive oil
2 garlic cloves, peeled and flattened with the side of a knife
8 large tomatoes (about 3 1/2 pounds), chopped
Salt and pepper to taste
1 teaspoon finely chopped fresh basil leaves or 1 teaspoon dried
1 pound spaghetti
1/2 cup grated Parmesan cheese

Peel the eggplant and slice it thinly. Arrange the slices in one layer on a large broiler pan and lightly brush the top of each with some of the olive oil. Set the pan under a hot broiler and brown the slices. Turn the slices over, brushing with olive oil, and brown the second side. Keep the slices warm.

In a large saucepan, heat the remaining olive oil (about 1/3 cup). Add the garlic cloves and brown, then remove and discard the garlic, leaving the garlic-flavored oil. Add the tomatoes, salt and pepper, and basil, and cook until they are reduced to a thick puree. Keep warm.

While the sauce cooks, boil the spaghetti in plenty of salted water until tender but still firm. Drain the spaghetti and place it on a deep serving platter.

Toss the sauce with the spaghetti. Sprinkle with half of the Parmesan cheese. Arrange the eggplant slices, overlapping each other over the spaghetti and cheese. Serve hot and pass the remaining Parmesan cheese at the table.

Richard Cicchi
Santa Barbara, California

Cavatelli con Rapini

(Shells with Rapini)
Yield: 6 servings

Cavatelli is a short, curled noodle, shaped like a shell. Rapini, or broccoli di rapa, is a pungent, somewhat bitter nonheading Italian spring green, a leafy broccoli that can be prepared and cooked like spinach.

1 pound rapini (or broccoli)
1 1/2 pounds canned whole Italian tomatoes with basil
1 pound cavatelli
4 tablespoons butter, cut into small pieces
Salt and pepper to taste
1 cup grated Parmesan cheese

Begin heating the water for the pasta.

Place the rapini in a saucepan with salted water. Boil until tender. Drain and keep warm.

Crush the tomatoes with your hands. In a saucepan, heat the tomatoes and the basil leaves with which they were canned to a simmer.

Boil the pasta until it is tender but still firm. Drain well, and transfer to a serving dish.

While the pasta cooks, add the rapini or broccoli to the tomatoes. Add the butter and salt and pepper. Pour the sauce over the pasta and serve hot. Pass the Parmesan at the table.

Angelo Verrico and Toni Musci
D'Angelo Trattoria
Laguna Hills, California

Porcini Sauce

(Mushroom Sauce)
Yield: About 2 cups

1/4 pound dried porcini mushrooms
3 sweet Italian sausages (or 12 ounces ground
  pork)
1 small red onion, finely chopped
1 garlic clove, minced
1 cup minced fresh Italian parsley
1/4 cup olive oil
4 tablespoons butter
1 tablespoon tomato paste
2 cups beef broth
Salt and pepper to taste
1 tablespoon all-purpose flour

Soak the mushrooms in 3 cups of hot water for 1 hour. Drain and save the water for a soup or sauce.

Remove the skins from the sausages, break up the meat, and combine well with the onion, garlic, and parsley.

Heat the oil and 3 tablespoons of the butter over medium heat; when the butter is completely melted, add the pork mixture. Saute for 5 minutes.

Dissolve the tomato paste in 1/2 cup of the broth. Add to the pork and cook for 5 minutes. Add the mushrooms and another 1/2 cup of broth. Season with salt and pepper. Reduce the heat and cook for another 30 minutes, adding the remaining 1 cup of broth as needed.

Mix the remaining 1 tablespoon of butter with the flour until completely blended. Add to the sauce and stir well. Cook for 5 minutes. Serve over hot tubular pasta.

David J. Holt
Italia
Seattle, Washington

Ragu alla Bolognese

(Bolognese Meat Sauce)
Yield: 6 servings

6 tablespoons butter
2 1/2 tablespoons olive oil
1 onion, finely chopped
1 carrot, finely chopped
1 celery rib, finely chopped
2/3 cup finely chopped bacon
3/4 cup minced pork
3/4 cup minced beef
1/4 cup sausage meat
2 to 3 chicken livers (optional)
2/3 cup dry white wine
Salt and pepper to taste
4 teaspoons tomato paste
1 1/4 cups beef broth
1/4 cup light cream or milk
Sauteed chopped mushrooms (optional)

Heat 3 tablespoons of the butter and all the oil in a deep frying pan. Add the onion, carrot, celery, and bacon. Fry until the vegetables begin to change color. Add the pork, beef, sausage, and, if desired, livers. Fry, crumbling the meat with a fork, until it begins to brown. Moisten with the wine and cook until the wine evaporates. Season with salt and pepper, then stir in the tomato paste and a little beef broth. Cover and cook slowly, stirring from time to time, gradually adding remaining broth.

After the sauce has simmered for 1 1/2 hours, stir in the cream and cook until the sauce is reduced. Add the remaining butter, and stir until the butter is melted and combined with the sauce. (If desired, sauteed chopped mushrooms can be added at this point.) Serve over tagliatelle.

Guiseppi Brunetti
Antico Brunetti
Bologna, Italy

40

Italo's Fettuccine Bolognese

(Fettuccine with Meat Sauce)
Yield: 2 servings

"This meatiest of the Italian pasta dishes is typical of the northern city of Bologna, where the art of good cooking and good eating is very appreciated," says Italo Carosiello, who provided me with this recipe. "The region is renowned for large farms yielding the best meats in Italy and the factories that preserve those meats as prosciutto (Italian ham), mortadella (Italian bologna), and an array of other goodies."

Tomato-Meat Sauce

1/4 cup olive oil
2 tablespoons minced onion
1/2 pound lean ground beef
2 tablespoons medium-dry white wine
3 cups tomato puree

Fettuccine

10 ounces fettuccine, preferably spinach
2 teaspoons butter
Grated Parmesan cheese

Heat the olive oil in a medium-size frying pan. Add the onions and saute until lightly browned. Add the ground beef, crumbling and stirring it with a fork until it is thoroughly cooked. Then slowly pour in the wine, add the tomato puree, and simmer for 10 to 15 minutes.

While the sauce simmers, bring the water for the pasta to a boil, salting it to taste. Cook the fettuccine, stirring lightly, until tender but still firm. Drain well, place in a serving dish, and quickly cover with the sauce. Top with butter and sprinkle with Parmesan cheese.

Italo Carosiello
Italo's Casa Romana
Seattle, Washington

Rigatoni con Salsicce

(Rigatoni with Italian Sausage)
Yield: 2 to 3 servings

3/4 pound hot Italian sausages
1/4 cup olive oil
1 green pepper, julienned
3 garlic cloves, minced
Leaves of 1 bunch basil, cut in slender ribbons
1 tablespoon chopped fresh oregano
1/8 cup finely julienned sun-dried tomatoes
Salt and pepper to taste
1 pound rigatoni

Preheat the oven to 350°F. Place the sausages in a shallow baking pan. Pierce each twice with a fork. Bake for 25 minutes. Remove the sausages from the pan and slice into 1/8-inch rounds.

Begin heating water for the pasta.

Heat the olive oil in a large frying pan. Add the pepper and saute for a few minutes over medium-low heat. Add the garlic and sausages and cook for 10 minutes over moderate heat. Add the basil, oregano, sun-dried tomatoes, and salt and pepper. Remove the pan from the heat and keep warm.

When the pasta cooking water comes to a full boil, add the rigatoni. Cook until tender but still firm, then drain the pasta and toss with the sauce. Taste for salt, and serve steaming hot.

Lucia Demeo
Pastabella
San Francisco, California

Linguine Puttanesca Marie

Yield: 4 servings

Executive Chef Mary-Jean George helped break down male resistance to hiring female chefs in Rhode Island with her repertoire of scrumptuous ethnic dishes such as this one. Puttanesca, "in the manner of a whore," is a fragrant, hearty tomato sauce said to have been invented by the prostitutes of Naples to lure prospective customers to their doors. The basic puttanesca should have olive oil, olives, garlic, anchovies, and capers—everything else is optional and to your own taste, "depending on whom you want to seduce," says Ms. George.

1/2 cup olive oil
1 small onion, chopped
4 ounces pancetta, finely chopped
1/4 teaspoon salt
1/2 teaspoon ground black pepper
2 teaspoons crushed hot red pepper
Dash cinnamon
1 tablespoon dried basil
1 tablespoon dried oregano
1 tablespoon dried thyme
Pinch dried tarragon
2 garlic cloves, minced
8 cups or 2 (28-ounce) cans peeled Italian plum
  tomatoes, crushed by hand
1 (12-ounce) can tomato paste
3 tablespoons pesto (see page 26)
3 ounces pine nuts
1 (3-ounce) jar capers, drained
3 ounces (3/4 cup) black olives, pitted and sliced
1 (4 3/4-ounce) jar marinated artichoke hearts,
  with liquid
6 anchovy fillets
1 tablespoon honey
1 pound linguine
Grated Parmesan cheese

Heat the oil in a large saucepan. Add the onion, pancetta, salt, black and red pepper, cinnamon, herbs, and garlic. Saute until the onion is wilted. Add the remaining ingredients, except the pasta and cheese, and simmer very gently for 1 hour.

Cook the pasta in plenty of boiling water until tender but still firm. Drain.

Serve the hot sauce over the linguine, and pass the Parmesan cheese.

Mary-Jean George
Gerardo's Supper Club
Providence, Rhode Island

Marinara Sauce

Yield: 6 to 8 servings

3 tablespoons olive oil
1 onion, minced
1 carrot, minced
1 celery rib, minced
3 garlic cloves, minced
6 fresh basil leaves, minced
1/4 cup minced fresh parsley
6 cups (6 pounds) peeled plum tomatoes, fresh
  or canned
Salt to taste
Sugar (optional)

In a large saucepan, heat the oil. Add the onion, carrot, celery, garlic, basil, and parsley and saute until the onion is limp, about 5 minutes. Add the tomatoes and salt, stir well, and cover. Bring to a boil, then reduce the heat and simmer for 30 minutes. Taste and adjust the seasoning. The sauce may need a pinch of sugar.

Ruby Ventimeglia
Brooklyn, New York

Stuffed
Pastas

These pastas are all made with homemade dough and then stuffed with meat or cheese or both. They take more time to prepare than the pastas in the previous chapter, but can be made ahead and held in the refrigerator or freezer.

In Italy, these pastas are served as a first course, before the meat. However, you will be tempted to make a whole meal out of one of these delicious recipes, and why not?

Tortelli d'Erbette

(Parmesan Tortelli with Green Stuffing)
Yield: 8 to 10 servings

These stuffed pastas are often made for special occasions, such as Christmas and New Year's. This recipe, which hails from Parma, is very typical of the tortelli of the region, with its stuffing of spinach or beet greens and its topping of melted butter.

This recipe was written for use with pastry flour. American all-purpose flour can be substituted, but since it is higher in gluten, you will probably need to use less.

Pasta

2 pounds (about 8 cups) pastry or all-purpose flour
6 eggs

Filling

1 pound spinach or beet greens
1 egg
1 pound ricotta cheese
Salt and pepper to taste
Pinch ground nutmeg

Topping

Grated Parmesan cheese
Melted butter

Pour the flour onto a smooth work surface and gather it into a mound. Make a well in the center. Beat the eggs and pour them into the well. Beating the eggs with a fork, gradually combine the eggs and four. Beat in 1/2 cup water, a little at a time, and knead thoroughly. Shape into a smooth round mass.

Wrap the dough in cloth and let it rest.

Begin heating water to boil the tortellini.

To make the filling, thoroughly wash the spinach or beet greens. In a saucepan, steam the greens until tender in the water that clings to the leaves after washing. Drain; squeeze out excess liquid. Chop the greens fine.

Beat the egg. Combine the egg, chopped greens, ricotta cheese, salt and pepper, and nutmeg. Refrigerate the stuffing mixture while you roll and cut the dough.

With a rolling pin, roll out the dough into a very thin layer and cut rectangles about 2 to 3 inches long and 1 to 1 1/2 inches wide. Place a spoonful of filling on each rectangle, and fold the rectangle in half. Press the edges firmly together to seal them.

When you run out of dough or filling, gently boil the tortellini for about 5 minutes, or until tender but still firm. Serve sprinkled abundantly with Parmesan cheese and melted butter.

Renato Baladelli
Ristorante La Filomena
Parma, Italy

Tortelli de Magro

(Lean Tortelli)
Yield: 8 servings

This recipe was brought to Cremona by the chef's grandparents from Busseto, in Parma, to be prepared at the Bissone, a restaurant that was established in 1500. Situated in the heart of Cremona near the highest bell tower in Italy, the Bissone is a popular gathering place in this hometown of Stradivarius. A varied clientele, including students from the violin-making school, come to sing, play music, and dance. During the Carnival in February, everyone wears fancy dress, great attention is given to candles, flowers, and decorations, and a warm, friendly atmosphere prevails. This dish was traditionally served on Fridays or other days of abstinence and the day before Christmas, as it contains no animal fat and is light and easy to digest. (*Giorno di magro* means day of abstinence in Italian.)

If you use all-purpose flour, you may not need as much. For the filling, I substituted ricotta cheese for the buttermilk curd the original recipe required.

Pasta

1 pound (about 4 cups) pastry flour or all-
   purpose flour
7 eggs

Filling

1 pound ricotta
3 1/2 ounces frozen spinach
1 egg
5 ounces Parmesan cheese, grated
Pinch nutmeg
Salt

Topping

Melted butter
Grated Parmesan cheese

Pour the flour onto a smooth work surface and gather it into a mound. Make a well in the center. Beat the eggs and pour them into the well. Beating the eggs with a fork, gradually combine the eggs and flour; if necessary, incorporate a little water. Wrap the dough in a cloth, and leave it in a cool place for about 1 hour.

Steam the spinach. Drain; squeeze out any excess water. Chop the spinach finely.

Place the ricotta in a bowl and add the spinach. Add the egg, Parmesan cheese, nutmeg, and salt; mix to a smooth paste.

Roll the dough very thin, in strips about 20 inches long by about 4 inches wide. Place a heaping teaspoonful of the filling every 2 inches along the pasta strips. Fold the pasta strips in half lengthwise, and press the edges to seal them firmly. Then cut the strips into lozenge shapes by making diagonal cuts between the mounds of filling.

Cook the tortelli in plenty of boiling salted water for 8 to 10 minutes; drain well.

Serve in heated dishes with melted butter and grated Parmesan cheese.

Vittorio and Jole Cremonini
Antica Locanda
Bissone, Cremona, Italy

Tortellini Suprema

Yield: 6 to 8 servings

Most Italian markets carry the two main ingredients to make this fabulous recipe—prosciutto and mortadella, the famous sausage of Bologna. For a sharper flavor, substitute Romano or Parmesan cheese for asiago.

Tortellini

1/2 pound prosciutto
2 thin slices (about 1/2 ounce) mortadella
1/4 cup grated Parmesan cheese
1/8 teaspoon ground nutmeg
2 egg yolks
1 1/2 recipes Pasta all'Uovo (see page 27)

Sauce

1/2 cup butter
2 tablespoons flour
2 cups whipping cream
1/4 teaspoon ground nutmeg
3 ounces (1 cup) grated asiago cheese

To make the filling, very finely chop the prosciutto and mortadella with a food processor or the finest blade of a meat grinder. Combine the meats with the Parmesan cheese, nutmeg, and egg yolks. Mix well.

Prepare the dough according to the recipe directions. On a lightly floured surface, roll out the dough into a rectangle about 1/8 inch thick. Cut the dough into strips 1 1/4 to 1 1/2 inches wide. Working with one strip at a time, cut it into squares. Put about 1/4 teaspoon in the center of each square. Fold the square in half diagonally to make a triangle, and press the edges firmly to seal them. Join the two ends of the long side of the triangle, overlapping them slightly and pressing them firmly together, to form a ring. Fold the remaining tip of the triangle toward this ring.

Begin heating a large pot of water to cook the tortellini.

For the sauce, melt the butter in a 2-quart saucepan over medium heat. Stir in the flour and cook until bubbly. Stir in the cream and nutmeg, and cook, stirring, until the sauce is smooth and thickened.

When the water comes to a rolling boil, drop in the tortellini and bring the water to a boil again. Cook the pasta gently, stirring occasionally, until tender (8 to 10 minutes); then drain. Place the tortellini on individual plates and pour the sauce over.

Richard Cicchi
Santa Barbara, California

46

Homemade Ravioli

Yield: 12 servings

Filling

1 carrot, chopped
1 celery rib, chopped
1 small onion, chopped
1/2 pound chopped fresh spinach
1 1/2 cups diced cooked chicken breast meat
1/2 cup chopped fresh parsley
2 garlic cloves, minced
1 teaspoon dried oregano
1 teaspoon dried basil
1/4 teaspoon pepper
1/4 teaspoon (or less) salt

Pasta and Sauce

Double recipe Pasta all'Uovo (see page 27)
12 cups Marinara Sauce (see page 42)
Parmesan cheese

Steam the carrot, celery, onion, and spinach in until just tender. Drain well.

Process the chicken and steamed vegetables to make a paste. Add the herbs and seasonings and mix well. Chill.

Prepare the pasta dough according to the recipe directions. Let it rest for 30 minutes. Roll into a large 1/8-inch thick rectangle on a large, flat, lightly floured surface. (A ravioli rolling pin and the kitchen table work well.) Spread half the dough with thin layer of filling (also about 1/8-inch thick) and bring the unfilled half of the dough over the filled half to cover it. Roll a ravioli rolling pin over it to mark the squares, or use a wooden yardstick. Cut ravioli apart with a pastry cutter.

Boil the ravioli gently in unsalted boiling water for 12 minutes. Drain carefully and serve with hot Marinara Sauce and Parmesan cheese.

Louis and Louise Dolceacqua
Hamden, Connecticut

Lumache Nona Ave

(Nona Ave's Snails)
Yield: 5 servings

This recipe for stuffed pasta shells originated in the town of Mazara del Valle in the northwest corner of Sicily. It was brought to this country by Mr. Greco's great-grandmother, Nona Ave, and is served at his inn.

1 1/4 pounds large lumache (shell pasta)
1 pound ricotta cheese
1/8 pound mozzarella cheese, grated
1/2 cup grated Romano cheese
1/2 cup fresh bread crumbs
1 egg
1/2 tablespoon chopped fresh parsley
Salt and pepper to taste
1/8 teaspoon dried thyme
1/8 teaspoon ground nutmeg
Tomato sauce

Cook the shells briefly in plenty of boiling water. Drain and rinse them.

Preheat the oven to 350°F.

In a large bowl, mix together the cheeses, bread crumbs, eggs, parsley, and seasonings. Stuff the shells with the mixture. Place the shells in a single layer in an oiled baking dish. Pour your favorite tomato sauce over them. Bake for 25 minutes. Serve hot.

Louis Greco
Leonardo's Italian Inn
San Diego, California

Seafood Lasagna

Yield: 6 servings

12 ounces lasagna noodles
2 1/2 cups Marinara Sauce (page 42) or red
  clam sauce
1 pound scallops
3/4 pound cooked small or medium shrimp
1/2 pound mushrooms (preferably canned),
  sliced
2 tablespoons chopped fresh parsley
1 pound provolone cheese (or mozzarrella),
  thinly sliced
1 pound ricotta cheese
5 to 6 large shrimp, with their tails, cooked
  (optional)
1/4 cup grated Parmesan cheese

Cook the lasagna noodles in plenty of boiling water until tender but still firm, and reserve them in ice water until needed.

Heat the sauce gently in a large pan.

Gently cook the scallops, a few at a time, by dropping them in boiling water for 2 minutes. Drain.

Add the scallops, small shrimp, mushrooms, and parsley to the warm sauce and stir to combine the ingredients. Spread a small amount of the sea-food sauce in the bottom of a 9-inch by 13-inch casserole. Arrange about a third of the lasagna noodles over the sauce. Spread a third of the sea-food sauce over the lasagna noodles. Top with a third of the provolone and ricotta cheeses. Repeat the layering two more times, garnishing the top of the lasagna with the large shrimp, if desired. Sprinkle Parmesan cheese over. Bake, uncovered, at 350°F for about 30 minutes; then serve.

Lawrence B. Cunningham
Italo's Restaurant
La Quinta, California

Lasagna Verdi alla Neapoletana

(Green Lasagna from Naples)
Yield: 12 to 15 servings

Pasta

1 egg white
1 tablespoon olive oil
1 tablespoon salt
1 1/2 cups all-purpose flour
3/4 pound fresh spinach leaves, blanched and
  chopped finely

Marinara Sauce

1/2 cup olive oil
4 cups coarsely chopped onions
2 small carrots, chopped (about 1 cup)
8 garlic cloves
1/2 pound pitted black olives
5 cups (35 ounces) peeled Italian tomatoes, with
  liquid
1/2 cup butter
1 tablespoon finely minced fresh parsley
1 1/2 teaspoons dried oregano
2 teaspoons dried basil or 2 tablespoons fresh
1 teaspoon dried thyme
1 bay leaf
Salt and pepper to taste
1 (6-ounce) can tomato paste (optional)

Cheese Layer

1 pound Italian provolone cheese, grated
1 pound ricotta cheese
1 pound mozzarella cheese (the kind made from
  buffalo is best), grated
1/2 pound Parmesan cheese, grated, plus 1/2
  cup for the top of the lasagna

To make the pasta, beat the egg white with the olive oil and salt. Pour the flour onto a smooth work surface and gather it into a mound. Make a well in the center. Pour the egg mixture and the spinach into the well. Beating with a fork, gradually mix the egg and spinach, then combine them with the flour. If necessary, incorporate a few drops of water. Knead thoroughly to make a smooth dough. Wrap the dough in a cloth, and let it rest for 15 minutes. Bring a large pot of water to a boil.

Roll the dough very thin and cut into strips 4 1/2 inches wide and 10 inches long. Cook the pasta in boiling water, 5 minutes or less, 2 or 3 strips at a time. Remove the strips, plunge them into cold water, rinse them in running water, and gently squeeze out excess water. Lay the strips on a towel to dry.

To make the sauce, heat the olive oil in a saucepan. Add the onions, carrots, garlic, and olives and saute until the onions are transparent. Puree the tomatoes in a food mill. Add the pureed tomatoes to the vegetables. Simmer 15 minutes. Set a sieve over a bowl and pour the sauce through; press with the back of a spoon to push the solids through. Return the strained sauce to the pan. Add the butter, herbs, and salt and pepper; simmer for 15 to 20 minutes. Remove the bay leaf. If the sauce is not thick enough, stir in some or all of the tomato paste.

Grease a 9-inch by 13-inch pan. Place a layer of lasagne noodles over the bottom. Alternate sauce and the mixed cheeses between layers of noodles until the lasagne is a couple of inches thick. The last layer should be noodles. Sprinkle the top with the remaining Parmesan cheese and bake at 375°F for 25 minutes.

Ellen Friebert Mershen
Afro-German Tearoom, Inc.
Louisville, Kentucky

Cannelloni Garibaldi

Yield: 6 servings

Cannelloni are stuffed tubes of pasta. These are filled with sweet Italian sausage, chopped spinach, and grated Parmesan cheese.

Dough for Pasta all'Uovo (see page 27)
1 pound sweet Italian sausages
1 (10-ounce) package frozen chopped spinach
1/2 cup finely grated Parmesan cheese
1 egg, lightly beaten
3 cups Marinara Sauce (see page 42)

Roll the pasta dough very thin, and cut it into rectangles 3 inches by 4 inches. Bring a large pot of water to a boil. Very briefly cook the pasta strips, a few at a time, then rinse them in cold water and lay them on a towel to dry.

Preheat the oven to 375°F. Remove the sausage meat from the casings and brown the meat in a large heavy skillet over moderately low heat for 10 to 15 minutes, stirring occasionally and breaking up large clumps with a spoon. With a slotted spoon, transfer the meat to a bowl.

Cook the spinach according to the package directions. Drain, pressing out as much water as possible with a spoon. Add the spinach, 1/4 cup Parmesan cheese, and the egg to the sausage; toss well to mix.

Butter a shallow 3-quart casserole. Divide the filling evenly among the pasta strips. Starting at one short end, roll up each of the strips, and arrange them seam-side down in a single layer. Spoon the sauce evenly over all and top with the remaining 1/4 cup Parmesan cheese.

Bake, uncovered, for about 30 minutes, until the cheese bubbles. Serve hot.

Ron Frieborn
Indian Wells, California

Rollatini alla Valle D'Aosta

(Rolled Lasagna, Valle D'Aosta-Style)
Yield: 6 servings

From the mountainous region of Italy that borders Switzerland comes this lasagna filled with spiced meat, currants, and pine nuts.

1/2 pound sweet Italian sausage
1 1/2 cups dry red wine
2 tablespoons olive oil
3 medium-size onions, minced
2 1/2 tablespoons minced carrot
2 bay leaves
1/2 pound lean pork shoulder, finely ground
1/2 pound lean beef chuck, finely ground
2 garlic cloves, minced
1/4 teaspoon dried marjoram
1/8 teaspoon ground cinnamon
1/8 teaspoon ground ginger
Generous pinch ground cloves
2 cups unsalted chicken or beef stock
  (preferably homemade)
1 tablespoon tomato paste
1/4 cup salted pine nuts
6 tablespoons grated Parmesan cheese
1 1/2 tablespoons minced dried currants
1/2 teaspoon freshly ground black pepper
1/4 teaspoon salt
12 lasagna noodles (flat, not ruffled)
1 cup whipping cream
Salt and pepper to taste
2 tablespoons shredded fontina cheese

In a medium-size heavy skillet, cook the sausage over medium heat until it is well browned on all sides, about 18 minutes; pierce several times to release the fat. Drain the fat from the skillet, and add 1/2 cup of the wine. Cover and simmer for about 30 minutes. Add a little water to the skillet, if necessary, to prevent sticking. With a slotted spoon, transfer the sausage to a small bowl; crumble when cool. Boil the liquid in the skillet until it is reduced to 1 tablespoon; then pour it over the sausage.

Heat the oil in a large heavy skillet over medium heat. Add the onions, carrot, and bay leaves. Cook until the onions are golden, stirring occasionally, about 10 minutes. Add the ground pork and beef, and cook until lightly browned, stirring occasionally, about 20 minutes. Add the garlic and cook for 30 seconds. Stir in the remaining 1 cup wine and the marjoram, cinnamon, ginger, and cloves, scraping up any browned bits. Simmer until the wine evaporates, about 5 minutes. Add the sausage mixture, 1 cup of the stock, and the tomato paste. Cover and simmer for 10 minutes. Uncover and cook until almost all moisture has evaporated. Cool to room temperature, and remove the bay leaves. Stir in the pine nuts, 4 tablespoons of the Parmesan cheese, and the currants. Add the pepper and salt.

Cook the lasagna noodles in plenty of boiling water very briefly, 5 minutes or less. Plunge them into cold water, rinse them in running water, and gently squeeze out excess water. Lay them on a towel to dry.

Preheat the oven to 350°F. Butter an 8-inch by 12-inch baking dish. Spread 1/3 cup of the filling in a 1/8-inch-thick layer over a cooked lasagne noodle, leaving a 1/4-inch border on all edges. Starting at one short end, carefully roll up the noodle to enclose the filling. Place rolled noodle seam-side down in the prepared dish. Repeat with the remaining noodles to fill the dish.

Boil the remaining 1 cup stock until reduced to 1/2 cup. Stir in the cream. Season with salt and pepper. Pour the mixture over the noodles. Combine the 2 tablespoons of fontina with the remaining 2 tablespoons Parmesan cheese, and sprinkle over the noodles.

Cover the dish with foil, and bake for 20 to 25 minutes. Uncover and continue baking until the cheese is bubbly, about 10 minutes. Let stand for 10 minutes before serving.

Andrea Sarti
Cavallo Bianco
Aosta, Italy

Lasagna alla Neopoletana

(Lasagna, Naples-Style)
Yield: 8 to 10 servings

1 pound ground or chopped meat (beef, pork, veal)
1/2 pound mild Italian sausage, chopped
1 cup chopped onion
1 cup chopped mushrooms (optional)
1 garlic clove, minced
3 cups tomato puree
1/2 cup dry red wine
1 bay leaf
2 teaspoons dried basil
1 teaspoon dried marjoram
1 teaspoon salt
1/4 teaspoon ground black pepper
10 ounces homemade or packaged lasagna noodles
2 eggs, beaten
2 cups ricotta cheese
1/2 cup grated Parmesan cheese, plus a little more for the top of the lasagna
1/4 cup chopped fresh parsley
1/2 pound mozzarella cheese, sliced

Begin heating water for the pasta.

In a skillet, cook the meats, onion, mushrooms, and garlic until the meat is brown. Drain off the fat. Stir in the tomato puree, wine, bay leaf, basil, marjoram, salt, and pepper. Bring to a boil, reduce the heat, and simmer, uncovered, for about 10 minutes, or to the desired consistency, stirring occasionally. Discard the bay leaf.

Cook the pasta in plenty of boiling salted water just until tender. Drain, rinse in cold water, and drain again.

Combine the eggs, ricotta cheese, Parmesan cheese, and parsley.

Grease a 9-inch by 13-inch baking dish and arrange some lasagna noodles in a single layer in the bottom. Spread with half the ricotta mixture, and sprinkle with a third of the mozzarella cheese. Cover with another layer of noodles, topped with half the meat sauce. Add another layer of noodles topped with the rest of the ricotta mixture and a third of the mozzarella, then a layer of noodles topped with the rest of the meat and most of the remaining sauce. Finish with a layer of noodles topped with tomato sauce. Cover the pan with foil.

Bake at 350°F for 30 minutes. Top with the remaining mozzarella cheese and a sprinkling of Parmesan. Bake for about 15 minutes longer, or until the cheese is melted and bubbly. Let the lasagna stand for 10 minutes, then cut into squares and serve.

Maria Grazia Benevento Dolceacqua
Salerno, Italy

Cheese-Stuffed Cannelloni

Yield: 6 servings

Cannelloni are sometimes made with crepes, as in this recipe, instead of pasta tubes. To save time, you can substitute 3/4 pound of manicotti tubes, cooked according to package instuctions.

Batter

2 eggs, lightly beaten
3/4 cup milk
1/2 teaspoon salt
1 cup sifted all-purpose flour

Filling

1 pound ricotta cheese
3 tablespoons grated Parmesan cheese
2 tablespoons minced fresh parsley
1 teaspoon salt
1 egg, lightly beaten

Topping

3 cups Marinara Sauce (see page 42) or Italian tomato sauce, heated
Grated Parmesan cheese

Preheat the oven to 350°F.

For the crepes, beat together the eggs, milk, and salt. While beating slowly, add the flour and continue to beat until the batter is smooth.

Grease a griddle and heat it to moderately hot. Drop spoonfuls of batter, 1 tablespoon for each crepe, onto the griddle, and allow the batter to spread into 4-inch-diameter circles. Flip the crepes when they start to brown and their edges begin to dry. Lightly brown the flip sides. Lay them on paper towels, lightest side down, as you cook the rest.

Mix together the filling ingredients.

Butter a 9-inch by 13-inch baking dish. Spoon about 1 1/2 tablespoons of the filling mixture on the center of each crepe. Then fold the top and bottom of the crepe toward the center, envelope fashion. Arrange the stuffed crepes seam-side down in the baking dish, and top with the heated sauce.

Bake, uncovered, for 30 minutes, or until bubbly. Serve hot with grated Parmesan cheese.

Lori Carangelo
Indian Wells, California

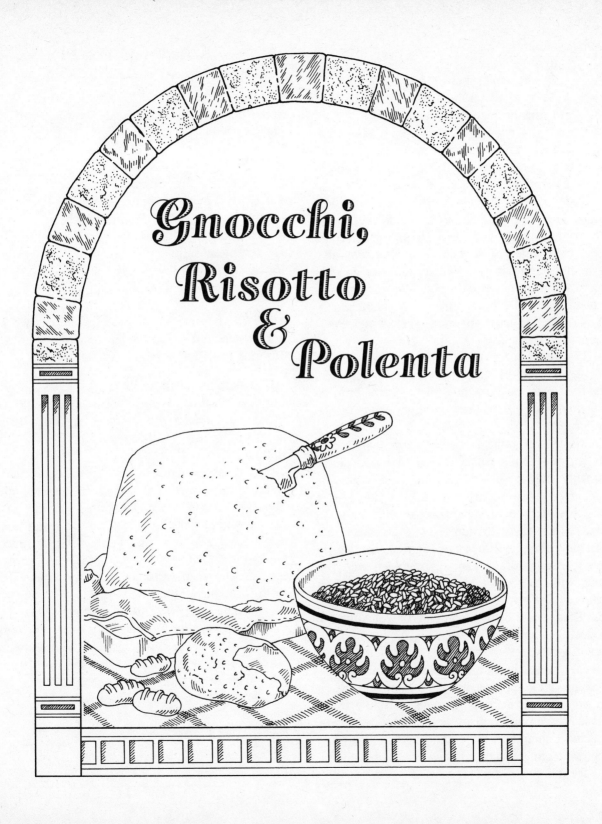

Gnocchi, Risotto & Polenta

Dumplings, rice, and polenta—dishes that might be served as side dishes in the typical meat-and-starch meal of the United States (if such a typical meal can be said to exist still)—are first courses in Italian cuisine.

Gnocchi (pronounced knee-O-key) is an ancient dish, first made under the name of ravioli. References to these simple dumplings are made in some of the oldest Italian cookbooks. Gnocchi can be made of various ingredients. In Emilia-Romagna you find *gnocchi verde*, made with spinach, eggs, cheeses, and flour. Roman gnocchi are likely to be made with coarsely ground semolina, eggs, and Parmesan. In Venice, look for gnocchi alla Cadorina, made with potatoes and smoked ricotta. Gnocchi zucca is made with pumpkin. By far, though, the most common type of gnocchi is made with potatoes.

The recipes for gnocchi appear simple, but making a good batch of gnocchi takes practice. The trick is to make the mixture stiff enough to be boiled without falling apart, yet light enough to be tender.

Risottos originated in the North, where rice has had a foothold since it was first introduced, probably in the fifteenth century. A risotto is made by slowly adding the cooking liquid to a special variety of rice, spoonfuls at a time, to produce a creamy mixture, yet with each grain remaining firm and separate. Of all the risotto dishes, risotto alla Milanese, a golden rice flavored with saffron, is the most famous. For best results, make risotto with arborio rice, as Italians do. This variety of rice, particularly well suited to producing a creamy risotto, is available at most Italian groceries. Uncle Ben's Converted Rice makes a surprisingly acceptable substitute.

Like gnocchi, polenta is a humble dish, a simple porridge made of cornmeal. While many Italians serve polenta plain or with a sauce, Americans most commonly allow the polenta to cool in a shallow baking pan, then they cut it into slices, and fry it.

Cheese Gnocchi

Yield: 4 servings

Serve hot as a lunch entree or as a substitute for potatoes with veal or chicken.

Gnocchi

1/2 pound ricotta cheese
1/2 cup all-purpose flour, sifted
6 tablespoons grated Parmesan cheese
3 tablespoons butter or margarine, melted
1/2 teaspoon salt
Pinch nutmeg
2 eggs, lightly beaten

Topping

1/3 cup melted butter or margarine
1/3 cup grated Parmesan cheese

Preheat the oven to 350°F.

Stir together all the gnocchi ingredients and spoon the mixture into a pastry bag fitted with a large pastry tube (with an opening of about 1/2 inch).

In a large kettle, heat about 5 quarts salted water to boiling, then reduce the heat to a simmer. Squeeze out the gnocchi mixture over the water, cutting with a knife at 1-inch intervals and letting the pieces drop into the water. Simmer, uncovered, for 2 to 3 minutes, until the gnocchi float, then remove them with a slotted spoon and drain them in a colander.

Arrange the gnocchi in a single layer in a buttered 1 1/2-quart shallow casserole, drizzle with melted butter, and sprinkle with Parmesan cheese. Bake the gnocchi, uncovered, for 10 minutes, then broil them for about 2 minutes, until they are lightly browned. Serve hot.

Maria Grazia Benevento Dolceacqua
Salerno, Italy

Gnocchi di Patate

(Potato Dumplings)
Yield: 4 servings

You are likely to encounter this classic in most trattorias in Rome. It is excellent as a side dish with chicken or veal.

3/4 pound russet potatoes, peeled
2 cups all-purpose flour
1/4 pound Romano cheese, grated
4 egg yolks
1 1/2 ounces butter
Salt and pepper to taste
1 to 2 tablespoons chopped fresh parsley
1 or 2 garlic cloves, chopped
Tomato, cream, or meat sauce, heated

Boil the potatoes for about 25 minutes until tender. Drain and mash them. Mix in the flour, cheese, egg yolks, and butter. Add the salt and pepper, parsley, and garlic. Knead all together until the dough is firm, though sticky.

Begin heating a large pot of water.

Shape the dough into long cylinders about 1/2 inch in diameter, and cut the rolls into 1/2-inch lengths. Press each one against the tines of a fork so that one side bears an indentation from your finger and the other side bears the mark of the fork. When the water comes to a boil, drop in the gnocchi, stirring carefully. They will rise to the surface when done. Remove them with a slotted spoon and place them on a serving dish. Pour the sauce over them and serve hot.

Franco Epifani
Lo Stivale Restaurant
Albuquerque, New Mexico

Gnocchi di Patate Fritti

(Fried Potato Dumplings)
Yield: 4 servings

These are an excellent accompaniment to roast chicken. The drippings from the chicken serve as sauce for the gnocchi.

1 pound potatoes, peeled
1 egg, slightly beaten
6 tablespoons butter
Olive oil

Boil the potatoes until tender. Drain them and mash them well.

Mix in the egg and butter.

Begin heating a large pot of water.

Shape the dough into thumb-size dumplings. When the water comes to a boil, drop in the gnocchi. Let them cook until they rise to the surface, then drain them well.

Put at least 1/2 inch olive oil in a deep skillet and heat. When the oil is very hot, slip in the gnocchi. Fry them until they are a uniform golden brown. Serve hot.

Ettore Benuzzi
Ettore Restaurant
Hindmarsh, South Australia

Risotto alla Milanese

Yield: 4 servings

There are dozens of risotti, soft rice mixtures that are to northern Italy what pasta is to southern Italy. This one is a classic, delicious with veal or chicken.

2 tablespoons butter
2 tablespoons beef marrow or 1/4 cup butter
1 small onion, chopped
1 cup arborio, short-grain, or Uncle Ben's
 Converted rice
2 cups hot chicken or beef broth or water
Pinch powdered saffron, or 1/8 teaspoon
 saffron threads soaked in 1/4 cup of the hot
 broth (strain and reserve the broth)
About 1/2 teaspoon salt
1/8 teaspoon freshly ground black pepper
1/4 cup grated Parmesan cheese

Melt the butter and marrow in a heavy saucepan over moderately high heat. Add the onion, and saute for about 1 minute, until it is a pale golden color. Add the rice and saute for 1 minute, stirring to coat it with the butter. Reduce the heat to moderate. Add 1/2 cup of the broth, the saffron, salt, and pepper. Cook, stirring constantly, until almost all the liquid is absorbed. While continuing to cook and stir, add the remaining 1 1/2 cups of broth, 1/2 cup at a time. Let the rice absorb the liquid each time before adding more. This will take 30 to 40 minutes. When the risotto is properly cooked, it will be creamy with just the slightest bite. With a fork, lightly mix in the cheese. Taste for salt, and serve.

Ron Frieborn
Indian Wells, California

Risotto con Vongole

(Rice with Clams)
Yield: 4 to 6 servings

If you don't have fish stock on hand, you can substitute shrimp stock made from boiling the shells, clam juice, or, even, broth made with fish bouillon cubes.

3 to 3 1/2 pounds baby clams in shell
Salt
5 tablespoons olive oil
2 garlic cloves, finely chopped
2 to 3 sprigs parsley, finely chopped
1 cup dry white wine
Freshly ground black pepper
2 1/2 cups arborio, short-grain, or Uncle Ben's
 Converted rice
6 1/2 cups boiling hot fish stock

Wash the clams thoroughly in plenty of salted water. Heat a heavy frying pan until very hot, add the clams, and shake them over the heat until they open. Cool and shell them.

Heat the olive oil in a large pan. Add the garlic and parsley, and saute until the garlic begins to color. Add the clams, reduce the heat, and simmer for a few minutes. Add the wine and cook until it evaporates; then season generously with pepper. Add the rice, stir gently, and cook until the rice begins to change color. Add a cup of stock and cook over moderate heat until it has been absorbed. Add the remaining 5 cups stock, a cup at time, until the stock is gone and the rice is tender. Taste for seasoning and serve immediately.

Carmen Cozza
Harry's Bar
Venice, Italy

Chicken Liver Risotto

Yield: 4 servings

1 pound chicken livers
6 tablespoons butter
1 large onion, minced
1/2 cup thinly sliced mushrooms
1 cup arborio, short-grain, or Uncle Ben's
  Converted rice
2 1/2 cups hot chicken broth
1/2 teaspoon salt
1/8 teaspoon freshly ground black pepper
2 tablespoons minced fresh parsley
1/4 cup grated Parmesan cheese

Halve the livers at the natural separation point, and pat them dry on paper towels.

Over moderately high heat, melt 4 tablespoons of the butter in a large skillet or flameproof casserole that has a tight-fitting lid. Add the livers and saute for 3 to 4 minutes, stirring until they are lightly browned. Remove them with a slotted spoon to a heated plate, cover, and keep warm.

Melt the remaining 2 tablespoons butter in the same skillet. Add the onion, and saute for 4 to 5 minutes. Add the mushrooms and saute for 5 minutes longer, until the onion and mushrooms are brown. Add the rice, broth, salt, and pepper. Mix well, and heat, uncovered, until the liquid begins to boil. Reduce the heat to low, cover, and simmer for 15 to 20 minutes, until the rice is tender. Stir in the livers, parsley, and Parmesan cheese. Serve.

Alfred Carangelo
Santa Barbara, California

Genoese Rice

Yield: 6 servings

2 cups short-grain white rice
2 cups chicken, veal, or beef broth
2 tablespoons butter
1 onion, thickly sliced
Handful chopped fresh parsley
2/3 pound veal, minced or diced
3 artichokes, trimmed and quartered
Salt and pepper to taste
Parmesan cheese, grated

Put the rice in a saucepan with a tight-fitting lid. Add the broth, cover, and quickly bring to a boil. Reduce the heat and let the rice simmer.

While the rice cooks, melt the butter in a large skillet. Add the onion and parsley, heat until the onions glaze. Add the veal and artichokes.

Preheat the oven to 450°F.

When the rice has absorbed about half the broth, add it to the veal mixture in the skillet. Cook over a low flame, stirring occasionally. Add a little more hot broth or water, if needed. Add salt and pepper and Parmesan cheese to taste. When the rice is ready (almost dry), pour it into a buttered casserole. Place the casserole, uncovered, in the oven. Remove it when a golden crust forms over the top of the rice. Serve hot.

Alvino Remmenga
Buellton, California

Suppli

(Rice Croquettes)
Yield: 6 servings

These suppli are Roman egg-shaped rice-balls stuffed with sauce, meat, and mozzarella. In southern Italy and Sicily, similar "rice oranges" are made.

2 cups short-grain white rice
1 teaspoon salt
2 1/2 cups Tomato-Meat Sauce (see page 41)
  or Ragu alla Bolognese (see page 40)
3 egg yolks, lightly beaten
Handful grated Parmesan cheese

Put the rice in a large saucepan with a tight-fitting lid. Add 4 cups water and the salt, cover, and bring quickly to a boil. Reduce the heat and simmer for about 15 minutes, until the rice is tender. Then spread out the rice on a wide plate or serving dish and let it cool.

Strain the meat sauce through a sieve onto the rice; reserve the bits of meat and vegetables left in the sieve. Add the egg yolks and Parmesan cheese to the rice and sauce, and mix carefully with your hands until the ingredients are well combined.

Heat the oven to 450°F.

Take a handful of the rice mixture and form it into a ball. Make a hollow in the middle, stuff the hollow with some of the reserved meat and vegetable bits from the sieved sauce, and seal with some of the rice mixture. Make more balls until all the rice mixture and stuffing is used.

Lay the balls on an oiled pan. Bake in the oven until the rice begins to brown. Serve at once.

Bob Milligani
Lancaster, California

Polenta con Fagiole

(Polenta with Beans)
Yield: 4 servings

My grandmother, Maria Grazia Benevento Dolceacqua, brought this traditional northern Italian cornmeal recipe from Salerno, Italy. It was handed down through 4 generations from Grandma to late Aunt Philomena and Uncle Frank, to Cousin Anna, and to Anna's children, Tina and Frank Jr.

1 (10-3/4 ounces) can condensed chicken broth
1 cup polenta (cornmeal)
8 tablespoons butter
Cooked cannelini beans (or white Italian
  kidney beans)
Grated Parmesan cheese
1 (15-ounce) can tomato sauce, heated
  (optional)

In a saucepan, bring the broth and 3/4 cup water to a boil. Reduce the heat and simmer.

In a bowl, blend 1 cup of water and the polenta until smooth. Pour the polenta mixture into the simmering broth, stirring constantly. Stir in 1 tablespoon of the butter. If desired, add the cannelini beans. Continue stirring over the heat for 20 minutes, or until the polenta comes away from the side of the pan as you stir. Then spoon the polenta mixture into a buttered bowl and let it stand 10 minutes.

Unmold the polenta onto a plate, and cut it into thick slices. Serve with the remaining 7 tablespoons butter and grated Parmesan. If desired, pour Italian tomato sauce over the slices.

Anna Arpaia Tropeano
North Haven, Connecticut

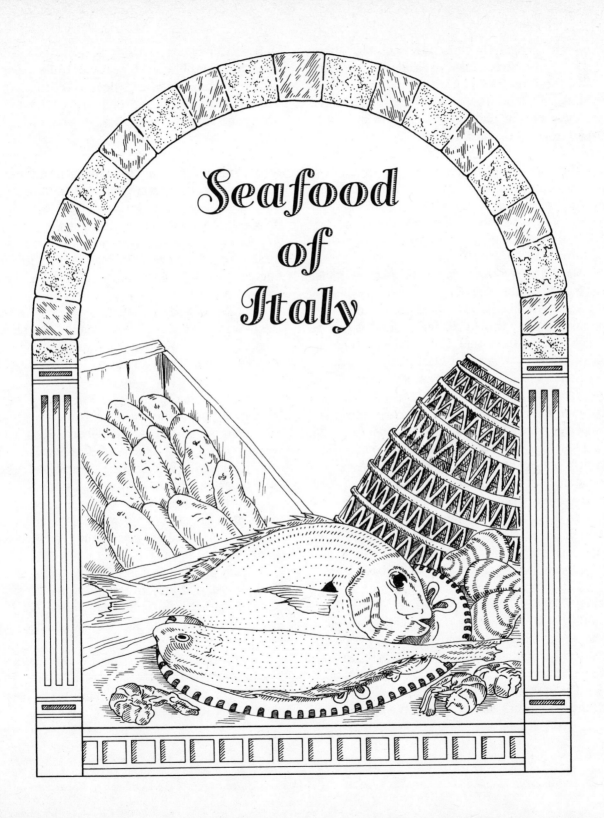

Seafood
of
Italy

The geography of Italy is such that almost every region has its share of coastline. Seafood ranks just behind pasta in its importance to the Italian diet. The Adriatic Sea and the waters around Sicily are two of the richest fishing regions of the Mediterranean, and the area provides some of the best seafood dishes in Italy.

There are so many Italian recipes for fish that it is difficult to make a selection; there are dozens of fish soups alone (see Chapter 3). The seven towns of the Marches region all claim the best *brodetto* (fish soup) of that particular stretch of coastline.

Nearly every sea creature is used in Italian cuisine. Even the dolphin, spared by the ancient Romans and Greeks, who considered it to be lord of the sea, is eaten by Italian sailors. It can be bought under the name of *musciame* at certain shops on the waterfront at Genoa and elsewhere.

Squid and octopus are two sea creatures that are common in Italian cuisine and relatively uncommon in the United States. If young, fresh, and properly prepared, these two can be exquisite; abused, they can be rubbery and tough. Both inkfish and tentacled, squid and octopus are prepared more or less the same way. Of the two, squid is the more delicate. The smaller they are, the better. They may reach awesome size (about 7 feet with tentacles extended). Canned and dried squid are sometimes available in specialty or ethnic groceries, and some squid is also sold frozen.

When cooking squid or octopus, plan to serve about 1/3 to 1/2 pound per person. The choicest squid weigh only a few ounces each. Octopuses are larger, the smallest weighing about 1 pound. For top quality, choose squid or octopuses that are firm and sweet-smelling with little or no liquid.

If your squid or octopus has not already been cleaned at the fish market, lay it on a counter back side up (the back is the side on which the eyes are most fully visible) with tentacles fully extended. With a sharp knife, cut down the center back, exposing the cuttlebone (a transparent bone that looks and feels like plastic). Lift it out and discard it.

Grasp the head and tentacles and pull toward you, turning the squid or octopus inside out and taking care not to rupture the ink sac. Save the sac, if you like, and use the ink in broth and stew. Discard all the other internal organs.

Remove the head, eyes, mouth, and parrot-like beak. Cut off the tentacles close to the head, pushing out and discarding the bead of flesh at the root of each tentacle.

Wash the body and tentacles several times in cool water. Squid is now ready for cooking, (though you can remove the skin if you want to). Octopus, unless very small and tender, must first be beaten.

If you dislike the purple skin of the octopus, remove it by placing the octopus in a large kettle of boiling salted water (1 teaspoon salt to 1 quart water), cover, and boil for 20 minutes. Then drain, plunge the octopus in ice water, and, using a stiff brush, scrub away the purple skin.

When choosing uncooked clams or mussels for a dish, discard any open or loose-shelled mollusks. After cooking, discard any mollusks that have failed to open.

When cooking seafood, do not oversalt. Add the salt last, and only to taste. The flavor of most seafood dishes will more fully develop if the dishes are allowed to sit for 15 minutes before serving.

The following recipes for fish and seafood are meant to be used for second-course dishes. To use seafood in antipasto, pasta, and pizza, see the chapters on these subjects.

Italian Baked Oysters on the Half-Shell

Yield: 6 to 8 servings

24 oysters in their shells, thoroughly washed
1 cup fresh bread crumbs
1/3 cup grated Parmesan or Romano cheese
1/4 cup minced fresh parsley
1/2 teaspoon dried thyme
1/8 teaspoon freshly ground black pepper
1/4 cup butter or margarine, melted
Rock salt (It retains the heat.)

Open each oyster and drain. Wash the deep bottom shells. Place each oyster in a bottom shell. Combine the bread crumbs, cheese, parsley, thyme, and pepper. Toss with the melted butter Spread the rock salt in the bottom of a shallow baking pan. Preheat the oven to 450°F. Top each oyster with about 1 tablespoon of the crumb mixture. Arrange the shells on the bed of rock salt. Bake for 8 to 10 minutes, or until the crumb mixture is lightly browned and the edges of the oysters begin to curl.

Alfred Carangelo
Santa Barbara, California

Cosmo's Steamed Clams

Yield: 6 servings

2 tablespoons olive oil
2 teaspoons minced garlic
72 littleneck clams, scrubbed and rinsed
5 3/4 cups (46 ounces) clam juice
1 (15-ounce) can crushed tomatoes
1 cup white wine
1/2 cup butter
2 teaspoons salt

2 teaspoons crushed hot red pepper
2 teaspoons dried oregano
2 teaspoons dried basil
2 teaspoons chopped fresh parsley

In a stockpot or dutch oven, heat the olive oil. Saute the garlic until golden. Add the remaining ingredients with 2 cups of water. Cover and boil, stirring occasionally. When most of the clams open, remove from the heat, and let stand for 5 minutes. Discard any clams that do not open. Place the clams in soup plates and ladle the broth over.

Tony Cosmo Calabrese
Cosmo's Underground Italian Restaurant and Lounge
Las Vegas, Nevada

Mussels and Clams Sicilian

Yield: 2 servings

10 mussels, scrubbed and debearded
10 clams, scrubbed and rinsed
1 tablespoon olive oil
1/4 teaspoon anchovy paste
1 teaspoon minced garlic
Pinch ground red pepper
3 to 4 teaspoons Chablis wine
Salt and pepper to taste
4 tablespoons Marinara Sauce (see page 42)

Steam the mussels and clams in a bit of water until they begin to open. Discard any that have not opened. Heat the olive oil in a small saucepan. Add the anchovy paste and garlic with the red pepper and saute for 40 seconds. Add the Chablis. Combine this mixture with the steamed mussels and clams, stirring it into the liquid in the pot.

Steve Warsh
Baci Seafood Ristorante
Palm Desert, California

Aragosta alla Catalana

(Catalan Spiny Lobster)
Yield: 5 servings

The spiny, or rock, lobster is smaller than the true lobster and has no claws. Overfishing has diminished its numbers in Italy, so it is becoming a rarity even there. You can substitute Maine lobsters or crayfish. Gianni Loche recommends serving this exquisitely simple dish as a first course, followed by a green salad dressed with olive oil, salt, and anchovies.

2-pound lobster
1/2 cup olive oil
1 large onion, minced
2 garlic cloves, minced
1 pound tomatoes, peeled
2 bay leaves
Pinch marjoram
Salt and pepper to taste
1/2 cup dry white wine

Cook the lobster in salted boiling water for 20 minutes. Remove the lobster from the pot and let it cool. Cut it into 10 pieces.

While the lobster cooks, begin making the Catalan sauce. In a medium-size pan, heat the olive oil. Add the onion and garlic. Saute until they are light brown, then add the tomatoes, bay leaves, marjoram, salt and pepper, and wine. Bring to a boil.

Put the lobster pieces in a baking dish and pour the boiling Catalan sauce over it. Let it rest for about 5 minutes. Serve with a dry Sardinian white wine, such as Giogantinu di Gallura or Aragosta di Alghero.

Gianni Loche
Rosticceria Azuni
Cagliari, Italy

Italo's Shrimp Pizzaiola
Yield: 2 servings

Italo created this dish for his wife, who loves seafood. The recipe is typical of the way fish is prepared along the southern coast of Italy.

2 tablespoons olive oil
2 tablespoons minced onion
2 tablespoons sliced fresh mushrooms
1 medium-size green pepper, chopped
16 medium shrimp (about 1/2 pound), shelled and deveined
Salt and pepper to taste
1/8 teaspoon dried oregano
1/8 teaspoon dried basil
1 small garlic clove, crushed
1/4 cup medium-dry white wine
2 fresh (or canned) tomatoes

In a skillet, heat the olive oil. Add the onion, mushrooms, and pepper and saute until they are half-cooked, just beginning to turn color. Add the shrimp, salt and pepper, oregano, basil, and garlic, and saute for about 5 minutes, until the shrimp are cooked. Slowly add the wine, then the tomatoes, crushing them with a fork and stirring. Simmer until the liquid is reduced by a third. Serve with hot Italian bread.

Italo Carosiello
Italo's Casa Romana
Seattle, Washington

Frittata alla Marinara

(Seafood Omelet)
Yield: 6 servings

4 to 5 tablespoons olive oil
1 garlic clove
1 pound mussels, scrubbed and debearded
1 pound clams, scrubbed and rinsed
12 oysters, scrubbed
1 pound medium shrimp in shell
6 eggs
Minced fresh parsley
Salt and pepper to taste

Heat 2 tablespoons of the oil in a large pan. Add the garlic and saute til golden, then add the mussels, clams, and oysters. Heat until most of the shells open. Let cool. Remove the shellfish from their shells, discarding any that did not open. Strain the broth and return to the pot. Bring to a boil and add the shrimp. Cook the shrimp until just tender. Remove and peel the shrimp. Strain the broth and set aside.

Beat the eggs with the parsley and a pinch of salt and pepper. Dilute with a tablespoon of the broth. Combine the egg mixture with the shellfish.

Heat 3 tablespoons olive oil in a frying pan. Cook the egg mixture over medium heat, turning once after the eggs have begun to set.

Antonio Cicchi
Ciro
Naples, Italy

Grandma's Prawns

Yield: 2 servings

1 cup olive oil
2 garlic cloves, crushed
10 jumbo shrimp, with tail, deveined
1/4 cup dry white wine
Salt to taste
1/2 teaspoon crushed hot red pepper
1/2 teaspoon dried oregano
10 black olives, pitted
2 medium-size ripe tomatoes, crushed
2 teaspoons capers

Saute the garlic in hot oil until it begins to color. Add the shrimp and cook for about 2 minutes, or until they redden. Add the wine, salt, red pepper, and oregano; stir and cook for another 2 minutes. Add the remaining ingredients, stir, and cover. Reduce the heat and simmer for approximately 6 minutes.

Ida Damiani
Mamma Vittoria Italian Restaurant
San Francisco, California

Cerino's Shrimp Saute

Yield: 4 servings

2 pounds shrimp, shelled and deveined
Flour to coat the shrimp
1 pound (2 cups) clarified butter
2 garlic cloves, minced
1 teaspoon salt
Lemons, quartered
1/4 cup chopped fresh parsley

Preheat the oven to 350°F.

Put clarified butter on the bottom of a pan. When the butter is hot, add just enough floured shrimp to cover the bottom of the pan. Cook for 1 minute on each side. Add a bit of the minced garlic and salt. Transfer the shrimp to a baking dish and keep warm. Repeat until all the shrimp are done. Squeeze lemon over the shrimp, sprinkle with parsley, and bake for 3 or 4 minutes.

Carrie Cerino
Carrie Cerino's Ristorante
North Royalton, Ohio

Shrimp Pancettati in Salsa Verde con Risotto

(Shrimp and Italian Bacon in
Green Sauce with Rice)
Yield: 4 to 6 servings

The secret to this recipe is using genuine Italian rice. Mr. Ilgrande prefers arborio rice, grown in the Po valley, but any imported Italian variety is fine. In a pinch, Uncle Ben's Converted Rice will do.

Salsa Verde

1 cup unsalted butter, at room temperature
Leaves of 1 bunch fresh parsley (preferably flat leaf)
Salt and pepper to taste
1/2 cup heavy cream

Risotto

1/2 cup butter
1 cup minced onion
1/4 pound fresh mushrooms, quartered (about 1 cup)
2 cups Italian rice
3 cups chicken stock
Salt and pepper to taste
1/2 cup grated Parmesan cheese

Shrimp and Pancetta

18 jumbo shrimp, shelled and deveined
18 thin slices pancetta
Salt and pepper to taste
About 1/2 cup all-purpose flour
1/4 cup olive oil

To make the sauce, combine the butter, parsley, and salt and pepper in a food processor, and process until the parsley is finely chopped and the ingredients are well blended. (Or chop the parsley by hand and pound it in a mortar. Gradually work in the butter.) Place the mixture in a bowl and freeze for 10 minutes.

While the herb butter chills, make the rice. Melt the butter in a large saucepan over high heat. Saute the onion and mushrooms for 3 minutes, or until the onions are soft and golden. Stir in the rice and cook for 1 minute. Add the chicken stock, 1 cup at a time. Bring to a boil and simmer uncovered, stirring, for 15 minutes, or until the rice is soft and the liquid is completely absorbed. Add salt and pepper. Press a piece of buttered foil over the rice to keep it warm until you ready to use it.

When the herb butter has chilled, bring the cream to a boil in a shallow pan. Gradually whisk in the herb butter until the sauce is creamy and foamy. Keep the sauce warm.

Preheat the oven to 350°F. Wrap each shrimp with a slice of pancetta. Lightly season with salt and pepper, and dust with flour. Thread the shrimp onto the skewers, 3 to a skewer.

Heat the olive oil in a large skillet, add the skewered shrimp, and saute for a few seconds on each side. Place the skillet in the oven for 2 to 3 minutes.

While the shrimp bakes, sprinkle the grated cheese over the rice, toss gently, and spoon the rice onto warm plates. Remove the shrimp from the skewers and arrange them on the plates. Pour the *salsa verde* over the shrimp. Serve at once.

Filippo Ilgrande
Il Tulipano
Miami, Florida

Naselli alla Marchigiana

(Hake in the Style of the Marches)
Yield: 4 servings

The variety of fish caught along the Marches on the Adriatic coast is astounding. As you might expect, this area is known for its fish recipes. Hake is a large seawater fish in the cod family. If you can't find hake at the fish market, substitute cod.

4 hake (or cod), about 1/2 pound each
Salt and pepper to taste
2 shallots, finely chopped
1 garlic clove, finely chopped
3/4 cup olive oil
About 1/2 cup dry bread crumbs
4 tablespoons butter
1 anchovy, rinsed, deboned, and chopped
Pinch potato flour
1 tablespoon red wine vinegar

Lay the hake side by side in a bowl just big enough to hold them. Sprinkle with the salt and pepper, the shallots, and the garlic. Pour all but 2 tablespoons of the olive oil over the hake, and leave them to marinate for an hour.

Prepare a grill for cooking the fish.

Remove the fish from the marinade, coat them with the bread crumbs, and sprinkle them with the remaining 2 tablespoons olive oil. Grill them on both sides over high heat.

While the fish are grilling, melt the butter in a small saucepan. Stir in the anchovy, potato flour, vinegar, and a little salt and pepper. Cook over low heat, mashing the pieces of anchovy with a fork until the sauce is smooth.

Serve the fish with the sauce poured over.

Anna della Salda
Da Carlo al Mare
Pesaro, Italy

Triglie all'Ancona

(Red Mullet from Ancona)
Yield: 4 servings

This recipe from the Marches combines red mullet with Parma ham. Prized by the Italians for its intense flavor, red mullet is often eaten ungutted: the liver is considered the best part. This is a very bony fish, which is why you often find it in *zuppa di pesce*, where the bones can be separated out from the broth. Native to the Atlantic Ocean, red mullet is sometimes available frozen in the United States.

4 red mullet, 1/2 pound each
Juice of 1 to 2 lemons
1 to 2 garlic cloves, minced
1 sprig rosemary, finely chopped
Salt and pepper to taste
2 sprigs parsley, finely chopped
About 2 tablespoons toasted bread crumbs
4 very thin slices prosciutto (Parma ham)
7 tablespoons olive oil

Whether or not you choose to clean the fish, scale them thoroughly. Rinse them, pat them dry, and place them in a dish.

Combine the lemon juice, garlic, rosemary, and salt and pepper. Pour the marinade over the fish. Let the fish marinate for 1 hour.

Preheat the oven to 300°F.

Stir together the parsley and bread crumbs. Coat each fish in this mixture, then wrap it in a slice of ham.

Strain the marinade into a baking dish just big enough to hold the wrapped fish side by side. Add the olive oil, lay the fish in the dish, and spoon the liquid over them. Place the dish in the oven and bake for about 25 minutes. Serve hot.

Aldo Lanelli
Miscia
Ancona, Italy

Torte di Pesce Spada

(Swordfish Pie)
Yield: 8 servings

A Sicilian dish. You can substitute halibut for the swordfish, if you like.

Pasta Frolla

4 cups all-purpose flour
3/4 cup superfine sugar
Pinch salt
1 cup butter
4 to 5 egg yolks
Grated zest of 1 lemon
Egg yolk

Filling

1 tablespoon olive oil
2 medium-size onions, minced
2 tablespoons tomato paste, diluted with 2
    tablespoons water
2 celery ribs, minced
3 to 4 ounces green olives, pitted and chopped
2 tablespoons capers
1 pound swordfish, finely chopped
Salt and pepper to taste
Oil for deep frying
4 to 5 small zucchini
1 egg
1/2 cup all-purpose flour

In a mixing bowl, combine the flour, sugar, and salt. Cut in the butter, and work the dough until the butter pieces are no larger than pea-size. Make a well in the center and add the egg yolks and lemon zest. Stir with your fingers until the ingredients are well blended and the mixture forms a ball. If the dough remains too crumbly, add a very little water. Wrap the dough in waxed paper, and leave it in the refrigerator for an hour.

To make the filling, heat the olive oil in a large saute pan. Add the onions and saute until they are golden brown. Add the tomato paste, celery, olives, and capers. Season the swordfish with salt and pepper and add it to the pan. Cook gently until the sauce is well reduced.

In a heavy saucepan, heat the oil for frying the zucchini. Cut the zucchini into 1/2-inch by 2-inch strips. Coat the strips with first the beaten egg, then the flour. Fry the strips in the hot oil; drain on absorbent paper.

Preheat the oven to 350°F.

Butter and flour an 8-inch torte pan with a removable rim. Divide the pastry into thirds. Gently roll the first piece into a circle slightly larger than the pan. Place it in the pan so it covers the bottom and comes partly up the side. Lay half the swordfish mixture and half the zucchini in this bed. Roll out a second pastry circle, and cover the swordfish and zucchini with it; add another layer of swordfish and zucchini. Top with a third pastry circle, making sure it reaches the side of the pan all around. Brush egg yolk over the top.

Bake for 50 to 55 minutes, until the pastry is golden brown. Remove the rim of the pan and serve the pie warm.

Emilio Loreto
La Cuccagna
Palermo, Italy

Brodetto di Mare Adriatico

(Adriatic Seafood Platter)
Yield: 4 servings

If you are in Los Angeles, a visit to Emilio's Ristorante is a must. The restaurant sprawls in all directions, including one that leads to a fountain and seven pillars, representing the Seven Pillars of Rome. Emilio himself plays the concertina for his customers.

This recipe hails from Emilio's native Abruzzi. Another of his specialties includes a whole barracuda baked in white wine.

1/2 cup olive oil
5 garlic cloves
6 tomatoes, peeled and crushed
2 pounds mixed seafood: cuttlefish (cleaned and beaten), squid (cleaned and skinned), red mullet (scaled and cut into chunks), clams (scrubbed and rinsed in several changes of water), mussels (scrubbed and debearded), etc.
2 tablespoons red wine vinegar
1 tablespoon chopped fresh parsley
Salt and pepper to taste

In a large pan, heat the olive oil. Saute the garlic cloves until they are golden. Add the tomatoes and cook for 3 minutes. Add the cuttlefish, squid, and clams, and continue cooking for 2 minutes. Add the remaining ingredients and cook for 4 minutes, then serve.

Emilio Baglioni
Emilio's Ristorante
Los Angeles, California

Antonino's Mackerel Porticello

Yield: 4 servings

A Sicilian specialty, great with fettuccine or by itself with tomato sauce or Marinara Sauce (see page 42).

3 tablespoons olive oil
2 onions, finely chopped
1 teaspoon minced garlic
5 anchovy fillets
2 tomatoes, chopped
1 pound mackerel, fresh or canned, skinned, carefully deboned, and cut into 2-inch pieces
3 tablespoons butter
1 pound fettuccine, cooked
6 tablespoons grated Pecorino Romano or Parmesan cheese
3 tablespoons minced fresh cilantro or parsley

Heat the olive oil in a large saute pan. Add the onions and garlic and saute until the onions are golden brown. Add the anchovies, tomatoes, and mackerel. Cook for 5 minutes, or until the fish is done. Add the butter; when it melts, the sauce is ready. (If you prefer a more liquid sauce, add 1/2 cup water and heat through.) Serve over hot fettuccine, and garnish with the cheese and cilantro. Or try it over spaghetti sauce or Marinara Sauce for extra flavor.

Antonino LoPiparo
Antonino's Sicilian Ristorante del Carrello
Milwaukee, Wisconsin

Sogliola Certosina

(Fillet of Sole Certosina)
Yield: 2 servings

2 to 4 tablespoons butter
4 medium-size fillets of sole (about 1 pound)
3 to 4 ounces jumbo shrimp, shelled and
  deveined
1 garlic clove, crushed
1/2 cup dry white wine
1 (15-ounce) can plum tomatoes, chopped
Salt and pepper to taste
1/2 cup heavy cream

Heat the butter in a large skillet and briefly saute the fillets on both sides to seal in the juices. Add the shrimp and garlic. Continue to saute for 2 to 3 minutes. Add the white wine; cook until most of the liquid has evaporated. Add the tomatoes and simmer gently. Season with the salt and pepper, then stir in the cream. Simmer until the liquid is reduced. Correct the seasoning and serve.

Leo and Linda Godini
Poldino's
Aberdeen, Scotland

Salt Cod with White Wine

Yield: 4 servings

2 pounds salt cod
1/2 cup all-purpose flour
1/2 cup olive oil
2 onions, chopped
1 cup white wine
Juice of 2 lemons
1/4 cup chopped fresh parsley
Salt and pepper
4 green tomatoes, sliced

Soak the cod in several changes of water for 24 to 36 hours. Prepare a grill for cooking the cod.

Divide the cod into fourths. Coat each piece with flour. Lay the fish on the grill and cook until they are white in the center and firm to the touch. While the fish cooks, prepare the sauce. Heat the oil in a saucepan. Add the onions and saute until golden. Add the wine, lemon juice, parsley, and salt and pepper, and cook for 10 minutes. To serve, spoon the sauce over the fish and garnish with slices of green tomato.

Marisa Sentuti
"G.B."
Rome, Italy

Casseruola di Pesce

(Fish Casserole)
Yield: 1 serving

1/4 cup olive oil
1 fresh whitefish fillet
2 large shrimp, in their shells
1/2 live lobster, cut into pieces
4 clams, scrubbed and rinsed in several changes
  of water
Several mussels, scrubbed and debearded
1 garlic clove, chopped
1 cup white wine
1 cup peeled whole tomatoes
Ground red pepper to taste
Chopped fresh parsley
Salt and pepper to taste

In a large pan, heat the olive oil. Briefly saute the whitefish on both sides. Add the shrimp, lobster, clams, and mussels. When the seafood is half cooked, add the garlic. Add the wine and cook to reduce it to half its original volume. Add the tomatoes and again reduce the sauce. When the seafood is fully cooked, season with the red pepper, parsley, and salt and pepper. Serve hot.

Gioacchino di Meglio
The Little Venice Restaurant
Hamilton, Bermuda

Scungilli Marinara

(Conch in Tomato Sauce)
Yield: 4 servings

Scungilli is the Italian word for conch, and marinara is a favorite Italian way of preparing it—with tomatoes, garlic, and onion. If conch is unavailable, substitute scallops.

2 tablespoons olive oil
1/2 cup minced onion
1 garlic clove, crushed
1 (15-ounce) can plum tomatoes, with liquid
1/4 cup tomato paste
1/2 cup dry red wine
1/2 teaspoon sugar
1 teaspoon salt
1 teaspoon dried oregano
1/8 teaspoon freshly ground black pepper
1 pound conch meat, sliced and poached for 20 to 30 minutes, or 1 pound scallops
2 teaspoons finely grated Parmesan cheese

Heat the olive oil in a large saucepan. Add the onion and garlic and saute over moderate heat for 8 to 10 minutes, until golden. Reduce the heat to low and add all the remaining ingredients, except the conch and cheese. Cover and simmer for 1 hour, stirring occasionally. (If the sauce becomes too thick, thin it with a little water.) Let the sauce cool slightly, then puree it in a blender or food processor. Return the sauce to the pan and add the conch. Cover and simmer for 3 to 5 minutes. Stir in the cheese. Serve hot over spaghetti or other pasta.

Louis and Louise Dolceacqua
Hamden, Connecticut

Misto di Pesce del Tirreno

(Mixed Fish from the Tyrrhenian Sea)
Yield: 4 servings

2 1/2 pounds mixed fish and shellfish: fillet of sole or sea bass, jumbo shrimp (in their shells), and crayfish or European lobster (cut into pieces)
1/2 cup white wine
1 tablespoon olive oil
Salt and pepper to taste
1/4 cup minced fresh parsley
1/4 cup minced fresh basil
1 small onion, minced

Preheat the oven to 425°F.

Oil a baking pan large enough to hold all the seafood, and lay the seafood on it. Sprinkle the seafood with the white wine, oil, and salt and pepper. Place the pan in the oven, and braise for 10 minutes, uncovered. Remove the pan from the oven, and sprinkle the minced herbs over the seafood. Return the pan to the oven for another 5 minutes. Serve hot.

Sergio Lorenzi
Ristorante Sergio
Pisa, Italy

Mediterranean Calamari

(Mediterranean-Style Squid)
Yield: 4 to 6 servings

You can substitute octopus for the squid.

2 tablespoons olive oil
2 medium-size yellow onions, minced
2 to 3 garlic cloves, crushed
2 pounds squid (cleaned and skinned) or
   octopus (cleaned and pounded), cut into
   2-inch chunks
1 (6-ounce) can tomato paste
1 cup dry white wine or dry vermouth
1/8 teaspoon crushed hot red peppers
1 tablespoon minced fresh parsley
Salt to taste

In a large saucepan, heat the olive oil. Add the onions and saute for 8 to 10 minutes, until golden. Add the garlic and saute for 1 minute. Add the squid, 1 cup water, and all the remaining ingredients, except the salt. Mix well, cover, and simmer for 45 to 60 minutes, stirring occasionally, until the squid is tender (the best way to tell is to eat a piece). Add salt. Serve over hot boiled rice.

Robert P. Turkington
San Francisco, California

Eel Stew

Yield: 6 to 8 servings

The average eel weighs 1 to 4 pounds; its meat is oily but mellow in flavor. Popular along the Mediterranean coast of Italy, eels are sold at market live, smoked, or canned. They can be baked, broiled, charbroiled, pan-fried, or poached.

2 (3-pound) eels
2 tablespoons clarified butter
3/4 pound small pearl onions
6 tablespoons all-purpose flour
1 cup brown stock
2 tablespoons red wine
Salt and pepper to taste
Minced fresh parsley

Cut off the eels' heads. Wash the eels thoroughly in cold, salted water, then soak them in clean water for 15 minutes. Skin, clean, bone, and rinse them. Cut them into slices 1 1/2 inches thick, and dry the slices thoroughly.

Melt the butter in a large saute pan. Add the onions and saute until golden. Sprinkle in the flour. Stir in the stock and wine; bring to a boil. Add the eel slices and salt and pepper. Simmer gently until the eel is tender, at least 30 minutes. Arrange the eel slices and onions on a serving dish. Strain the sauce over the fish and garnish with parsley. Serve hot.

Robert P. Turkington
San Francisco, California

Poultry has been preferred to red meat in the Italian diet for centuries. Chicken, turkey, capons, and squabs, as well as game birds, are found on menus throughout the country.

Until recently, chicken was food for the rich. Chickens were kept primarily for their eggs, and the flesh was eaten only when the bird was too old to be a productive layer. Nonetheless, the enormous number of distinctively Italian chicken dishes is staggering. Chicken is broiled, baked, stewed, and cooked on a spit. It is cooked with innumerable sauces that change a simple dish to an elaborate one. Chicken breasts are scallopined (boned and pounded), breaded, sauteed, and combined with a rich sauce of Marsala wine and cream. A favorite cooking method is pan-roasting.

Turkey was introduced into Europe from North America by the Spaniards in the sixteenth century. In the Lombardy and Piedmont regions of Italy, a traditional Christmas dinner is roast turkey stuffed with a mixture of chestnuts, sausage, truffles, apples, and prunes.

Pollo Ripieno alla Lucana

(Stuffed Chicken Lucania Style)
Yield: 3 to 4 servings

4 tablespoons lard or butter
4 to 5 chicken livers
Salt and pepper to taste
2 eggs
4 tablespoons grated Pecorino Romano cheese
2 1/2 pound chicken, washed and patted dry
1 to 2 sprigs fresh sage (optional)
1 sprig fresh rosemary (optional)

Preheat the oven to 375°F.

Heat 1 tablespoon of the lard in a small pan. Add the livers and a pinch of salt and pepper and saute gently for 5 minutes. Remove from the heat and chop the livers finely; set aside.

Beat the eggs. Mix the eggs with the cheese and the livers.

Sprinkle the cavity of the chicken with salt, and stuff it with the cheese mixture. Insert the sage and rosemary, if desired. Sew up the opening, and truss or tie the chicken. Rub the outside of the chicken with the 3 remaining tablespoons of the lard, and sprinkle with salt and freshly ground pepper. Put the chicken in a roasting pan. Roast for about 1 hour, turning the chicken occasionally and basting it with the pan juices.

Cut the chicken into serving portions and serve with the pan juices.

Gianni Guido
Guido
Lecce, Italy

Pollo alla Vesuvio

(Chicken in the Style of Vesuvius)
Yield: 4 servings

Today it's restaurant fare, but Mr. Riccio says he learned to make this simple chicken dish by watching his grandmother prepare it. The chicken is richly flavored with garlic and Marsala. A bit of red pepper gives it a glow that makes it worthy to be named after Vesuvius, a still-active volcano situated east of the Bay of Naples.

2 chickens, washed and patted dry
1/4 cup olive oil
4 garlic cloves, crushed
4 teaspoons minced garlic
1/4 teaspoon salt
Freshly ground black pepper to taste
Ground red pepper to taste
1/4 cup Marsala wine
1/4 cup chicken stock
1 teaspoon finely chopped Italian parsley

Preheat the oven to 450°F. Cut each chicken in half, then cut each half into 8 pieces.

Heat the olive oil in a heavy ovenproof skillet over high heat. Add the crushed garlic cloves and cook until lightly browned. Add the chicken pieces and fry until they are brown and crisp on both sides. Place the skillet in the oven for approximately 15 minutes. Remove the skillet from the oven, drain off the oil, and remove the garlic cloves. Add the minced garlic, salt, and black and red pepper. Place the skillet on the stove over high heat until the garlic is browned. Add the Marsala and chicken stock. Continue cooking until the wine and stock are absorbed. Garnish with the parsley and serve.

Anthony L. Riccio
Riccio's
Palm Springs, California

Chicken Bianco
Yield: 3 to 4 servings

Dishes prepared in the *bianco* style are particularly light. Here, succulent slices of chicken, sausage, onion, and green bell peppers are sauteed in a delicate mixture of pimiento, oregano, parsley, garlic, and wine.

1/2 cup butter
6 medium-size chicken breast halves, cut into
   1-inch slices
12 ounces sweet Italian sausage, sliced
2 medium-size onions, sliced
1 medium-size green pepper, sliced
1 (8-ounce) can pimientos, sliced
1 teaspoon dried oregano
1 1/2 teaspoons minced fresh parsley
3 garlic cloves, minced
2 tablespoons white wine

In a deep frying pan, melt the butter. Add the chicken slices, sausage, onions, and green pepper and saute until the onions are translucent. Add the pimientos, oregano, parsley, garlic, and white wine. Simmer for 8 minutes, and serve.

Al Borini
Scanniccuio's
Atlantic City, New Jersey

Pollo Calabrese

(Chicken, Calabria Style)
Yield: 2 servings

1/2 chicken, cut into serving pieces
3 tablespoons olive oil
1 garlic clove
1/2 cup quartered mushrooms
6 green olives (not pitted)
1/4 cup butter
6 tablespoons white wine
4 bay leaves
1/2 teaspoon dried rosemary
1/2 teaspoon dried thyme
1/4 teaspoon salt
Freshly ground black pepper to taste

Preheat the oven to 350°F. Lay the chicken pieces in a baking pan, and bake for 25 minutes.

In a large pan, heat the olive oil. Add the garlic and brown over high heat. Add the chicken, mushrooms, and olives, and mix. Add the butter and white wine, and bring to a boil. Add 6 tablespoons water, the bay leaves, herbs, salt, and pepper. Return to a boil and boil for 2 minutes. Cover and simmer for 20 minutes. Serve.

Michele Riccio
Rudy's Ristorante Italiano and Pizzeria
Seattle, Washington

Baked Chicken Giovanna

Yield: 4 to 6 servings

A simple, tasty chicken dish.

Marinade
3/4 cup olive oil
1 cup sherry
1 tablespoon crushed garlic
1 tablespoon dried oregano
1 tablespoon salt
1/2 tablespoon black pepper

Chicken
3-pound chicken, cut into pieces
Paprika

Mix the marinade ingredients. Pour half the marinade into a shallow baking pan and arrange the chicken pieces in the pan, skin side down. Pour the remaining marinade over the chicken. Allow the chicken pieces to marinate for at least 30 minutes.

Preheat the oven 350°F.

Place the pan with the chicken and marinade in the hot oven. Bake for 1 hour. Turn the pieces after 30 minutes. About 5 minutes before the chicken is done, sprinkle it lightly with paprika. Serve hot.

John H. Willis
Mario's Italian Cellar
Sacramento, California

Sicilian Chicken with Mint and Almonds

Yield: 4 servings

The assertive flavors of the Middle East, typical of the Sicilian kitchen, radiate from this dish.

1/4 cup fresh mint leaves, tightly packed
1 large garlic clove
3 1/2 pound chicken, quartered
3 tablespoons lemon juice
3 1/2 tablespoons olive oil
1/4 teaspoon freshly ground pepper
1 medium-size lemon
Salt
1/3 cup blanched whole almonds
2 tablespoons white wine vinegar
1 tablespoon minced fresh mint leaves
Mint sprigs

Mince together the 1/4 cup mint leaves and the garlic clove. Rub the chicken pieces with the mixture. Arrange the chicken pieces in a single layer in a shallow dish.

In a small bowl, combine the lemon juice, 1 tablespoon of the olive oil, and the pepper. Pour the marinade over the chicken and turn the pieces to coat them evenly. Cover the dish and refrigerate it for at least 5 hours, or overnight.

Using a sharp knife, cut very thin strips of the rind from the lemon, and boil them in water to cover for 5 minutes. Drain.

Remove the chicken from the dish. Scrape the mint mixture off the chicken and into the marinade. Reserve the marinade. Pat the chicken dry, and salt it lightly.

Heat the remaining 2-1/2 tablespoons olive oil in a large heavy skillet over medium heat. Add the almonds and saute until they are golden, stirring frequently. Remove them with a slotted spoon.

Add the chicken to the skillet, and brown it well on all sides. Stir in the vinegar, scraping up the browned bits from the bottom of the pan. Add the lemon peel and the reserved marinade. Reduce the heat, cover, and cook for 15 minutes. Add the almonds and 1 tablespoon mint leaves. Cover and cook, turning occasionally, until the chicken is tender, 10 to 15 minutes. (Add water if necessary to prevent the chicken from sticking to the pan.)

Transfer the chicken to a heated platter, and pour the pan juices over. Garnish with mint sprigs, and serve.

Silvio Parelli
Pippo Nunnari
Messina, Italy

Pollo alla Cacciatore

(Chicken in the Hunter's Style)
Yield: 4 servings

Chicken alla Cacciatore is a famous dish from central Italy. The chicken is first browned and then slowly cooked with mushrooms onions, celery, carrots, and herbs. Sometimes, as in this recipe, tomatoes are added.

2-pound to 3-pound chicken, cut into pieces
Flour
1/2 cup olive oil
1/2 cup minced onion
1 garlic clove, chopped
1 cup chopped celery
1 large green bell pepper, chopped
1 (15-ounce) can tomatoes, crushed
1 (8-ounce) can tomato sauce
1/4 cup chopped fresh parsley
1 bay leaf
1 (4-ounce) can button mushrooms

Dredge the chicken pieces in the flour. Heat the oil in a large skillet, add the chicken, and brown on all sides. Remove the chicken pieces with a slotted spoon and set them aside.

In the same oil, brown the onion, celery, and bell pepper. Stir in the tomatoes and the tomato sauce. Return the chicken to the pan and add the parsley and the bay leaf. Simmer for 30 minutes. Add the mushrooms, and simmer for 10 more minutes. Serve hot.

Andretta Brunetti
Savute's Italian Ristorante
Wichita, Kansas

Petto di Pollo Vicontessa

(Vicontessa's Breast of Chicken)
Yield: 4 servings

A family recipe from Abbiategrasso, Milan, enjoyed today in Canada. Serve the chicken over fettuccine or rice (mixed with butter and Parmesan cheese), or with a vegetable. Dry white wine is an excellent complement to this dish.

3 tablespoons olive oil
1 cup sliced button mushrooms
2 tablespoons butter
2 whole chicken breasts, boned, skinned, and pounded into 12-inch-thick scallops
3 tablespoons cognac
6 tablespoons Marsala wine
6 tablespoons chicken broth
Salt and pepper to taste
2 tablespoons julienned pimiento
Juice of 1/2 lemon
3/4 cup heavy cream

Heat 1 tablespoon of the olive oil in a small skillet. Add the mushrooms and saute until limp. Set them aside.

Heat the remaining 2 tablespoons olive oil and the butter almost to the smoking point in a large shallow pan over medium heat. Gently slip the chicken pieces into the pan and brown them completely on both sides. When they are golden brown, pour off the fat. Then pour the cognac and Marsala wine into the pan. With a match, light the liquor and flame the chicken until the fire goes out. Add the chicken broth. Season with the salt and pepper. Over medium heat, reduce the liquid by half. Add the mushrooms, pimiento, lemon juice, and cream. Simmer for a few minutes, until the sauce is a desirable consistency. Serve.

Bruno Chicchini
Bruno's Italian Restaurant
Edmonton, Alberta, Canada

Petti di Pollo al Spinacci e Formaggio

(Breasts of Chicken with
Spinach and Cheese)
Yield: 4 servings

While traveling through Ireland, I had a splendid dinner at Maryse and Gilbert's Restaurant, which is situated outside of Corofin Village, over the River Fergus. The restaurant is renowned for its French and Italian cuisine and has achieved special recognition from the *Board Failte* (Irish Tourist Board). This recipe comes from San Remo, in the Liguria Region of northern Italy.

4 large chicken breasts (or 8 small), skinned
1 pound spinach, unevenly cut with scissors
12 to 14 ounces Parmesan cheese, grated
1/4 cup olive oil
2 garlic cloves, minced
Salt, pepper, and paprika to taste
Juice of 1/2 lemon
1 cup dry white wine
Chopped flat-leafed parsley

With a sharp knife, slice the breasts lengthwise to form a pocket. Fill each breast with a portion of the spinach and the Parmesan cheese.

In a large skillet, heat the oil over moderate heat. Add the chicken and brown the breasts on both sides, occasionally turning gently. Sprinkle with the garlic, salt, pepper, and paprika. Turn a few times, and add the lemon juice and wine. Cover and cook for 30 to 35 minutes.

Serve garnished with parsley. Risotto alla Milanese goes well with this dish.

Maryse Mensile
Maryse and Gilbert's Restaurant
Corofin, County Clare, Republic of Ireland

Philip's Chicken Angelo

Yield: 6 servings

A tangy lemon chicken flambe.

3 whole chicken breasts, boned and cut into 4
  pieces each
Flour
6 tablespoons clarified butter
Dash dried oregano
Dash dried basil
Salt and pepper to taste
1/3 cup dry white wine
Juice of 1/2 to 1 small lemon
2 garlic cloves, minced
1 cup sliced mushrooms
6 (canned or frozen) artichoke hearts,
  quartered
1 tablespoon chopped fresh parsley
3/4 cup brandy

Dredge the chicken pieces in flour and shake off any excess. Heat 4 tablespoons of the clarified butter in a large skillet over medium heat. When the butter is hot, add the chicken and brown on all sides. Add the oregano and basil, and season with the salt and pepper. Add the remaining 2 tablespoons of the clarified butter to the skillet. When the butter is hot, add the wine, lemon juice, and garlic. Reduce the heat and simmer for 4 to 5 minutes. Add the mushrooms, artichoke hearts, and parsley. Cook until the mushrooms are tender, about 3 minutes. Turn the heat to high and add the brandy. Heat the brandy and ignite it with a match. Let the flames die down, then serve at once.

Philip Q. Deale
Philip's Supper House
Las Vegas, Nevada

Involtini di Petti di Pollo

(Stuffed Chicken Breasts)
Yield: 6 servings

Chicken breasts are stuffed with cheese and asparagus and smothered with a mushroom cream sauce.

12 (6-ounce) boneless chicken breast halves, skinned and trimmed
12 thin slices prosciutto
3/4 pound Bel Paese cheese, cut into 12 oblongs
24 asparagus spears, blanched 1 minute and trimmed to 4 inches
3/4 pound (total) Parmesan and Romano cheese, grated and mixed
1/2 cup minced fresh parsley
Olive oil
Flour
1 pound mushrooms, thinly sliced
3/4 cup dry Marsala wine
6 cups heavy cream
Salt and pepper to taste

Pound the chicken breasts between sheets of waxed paper to a thickness of 1/4 inch. Lay them shiny side down, and cover each breast with 1 prosciutto slice. Set a Bel Paese cheese oblong in the center, and place 2 pieces of asparagus beside the cheese. Sprinkle with about 3 tablespoons of the Parmesan-Romano mixture, then with the parsley. Tightly roll up the breasts.

Preheat the oven to 350°F.

In a large heavy skillet, heat a thin layer of oil over medium heat. Dredge the chicken rolls in the flour, shaking off any excess. Arrange the rolls seam side down in the skillet and brown them on both sides. Transfer them to a baking sheet. Pour the oil from the pan over them. (Do not wash the skillet.) Bake the chicken until it is tender, about 15 minutes.

While the chicken bakes, set the skillet over high heat, and add the mushrooms and Marsala wine. Tilt the pan, heat the wine and ignite it with a match. When the flame subsides, boil the liquid until it is reduced by half. Add the cream, and boil it until the sauce is reduced to a desirable consistency. Season with salt and pepper.

To serve, set 2 chicken rolls on each plate, and spoon the Marsala sauce over.

Jacquiline Armstrong
Lofurno's
Seattle, Washington

Rollatini di Pollo Don Fosco

(Fosco's Stuffed Chicken Breast)
Yield: 4 servings

A recipe that originated in the Tuscany region of Italy.

8 large boneless chicken breast halves, skinned and trimmed
1/2 pound ground pork
1/2 medium-size onion, chopped
1/3 cup crumbled cooked bacon bits
2 garlic cloves, chopped
1 egg
1/2 cup fresh white bread crumbs
1/2 teaspoon salt
1/4 teaspoon freshly ground black pepper
Dried basil, oregano, and sage to taste
1/4 cup cooked chopped spinach
2 teaspoons butter, melted
Salt and pepper to taste
1/2 cup Marsala wine
1 cup brown stock
Chopped fresh parsley

Pound the chicken breasts between sheets of waxed paper to a thickness of 1/4 inch.

Preheat the oven to 400°F.

In a skillet, begin frying the ground pork. Add the onion, bacon, and garlic, and cook until all are brown. Drain the fat from the skillet. Stir in the egg, bread crumbs, salt and pepper, herbs, and spinach. Mix well.

Place equal portions of stuffing on each chicken breast. Roll up the breasts, and secure the rolls with toothpicks. Place the rolls, seam side down, in a greased baking pan, and brush them with the butter. Sprinkle them with salt and pepper. Pour the Marsala wine over, and bake for 35 to 40 minutes.

Remove the pan from the oven and the rolls from the pan. Stir the brown stock into the pan juices, and return the pan to the oven for 5 more minutes. Replace the rolls in the resulting sauce, and sprinkle them with the parsley. Serve the rolls with the sauce and mashed potatoes or polenta.

Hugo Baumann
Il Palio Ristorante
Somerset, Bermuda

Pollo alla Fiorentina

(Florence-Style Chicken)
Yield: 4 servings

At Mario's, where I dined on this elegant dish, a superb operatic chorus of waiters and waitresses sing while you dine.

2 (2 1/4-pound to 2 1/2-pound) chickens, halved
1/4 pound ground Italian sausage
1/4 pound spinach, chopped, cooked, and
  drained
1/2 cup butter
2 tablespoons chopped shallots
Dash dry vermouth
Salt and pepper to taste

Remove the chicken wings (reserve them for stock or another use). Carefully separate each chicken breast half from the bone, all the way down to the thigh. Roll back the meat on the thigh to remove the thigh bone without puncturing the skin. This will leave only the drumstick bone attached to the meat.

In a small skillet, cook the Italian sausage; drain off the fat. Stir in the spinach.

In a separate pan, melt the butter. Saute the shallots lightly, and stir in the sausage-spinach mixture. Add the vermouth, salt, and pepper. Mix well. Let the stuffing cool.

Preheat the oven to 400°F.

Place a portion of the stuffing on the boned side of each chicken half. Mold the meat around the stuffing, overlapping the sides, to form a pear shape, with the drumstick sticking up. Place the chicken halves seam side down on a greased roasting pan, and bake until they are done, about 1 hour. Serve.

Mario Lalli
Mario's Restaurant
Rancho Mirage, California

Pollo alla Gorgonzola

(Chicken with Gorgonzola Cheese)
Yield: 2 servings

1/4 pound Gorgonzola cheese, crumbled
White wine
6 ounces cubed chicken breast
Flour
1/4 cup butter
2 scallions, sliced
1/3 cup sliced mushrooms
3/4 cup cream
5 tablespoons grated Parmesan cheese
Salt and pepper to taste
2 1/2 ounces fettuccine
Chopped fresh parsley

Begin heating the water for the pasta. Place the Gorgonzola in a glass or ceramic bowl and cover with the white wine. Set aside.

Dredge the chicken in flour; shake off any excess. In a skillet, melt the butter. Add the chicken and saute for 1 minute. Add the scallions and mushrooms and saute until the mushrooms are limp, about 5 minutes. Add the Gorgonzola mixture, the cream, Parmesan cheese, and salt and pepper. Heat, stirring, until the cream thickens. Reduce the heat to very low.

When the cream has thickened and the water for the pasta has reached a full boil, drop the fettuccine into the boiling water. Boil until the pasta is tender but still firm; drain. Place the cooked fettuccine on a platter, top with the chicken. Garnish with the parsley and serve.

William Kavadias
Toscanini
Washington, D.C.

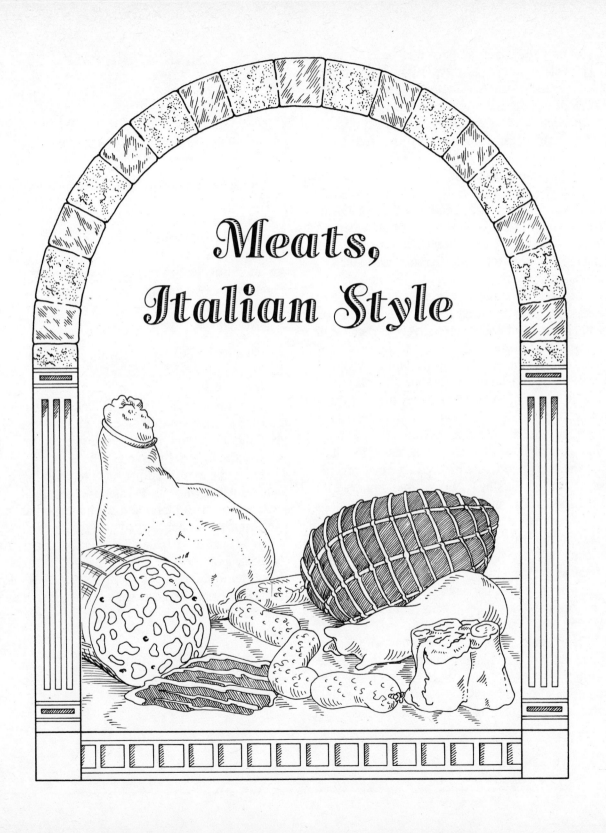

Meats,
Italian Style

The Italians are not known to be great meat eaters; nonetheless typical trattoria menus include delicious offerings of veal and pork and, occasionally, beef, lamb, and rabbit.

Milk-fed veal is probably the most popular meat in Italy. Veal can be sauteed, braised, fried, stewed, roasted, or poached. Ossobuco alla Milanese (Braised Veal Shanks in the style of Milan) is a popular braised veal dish. Veal shank is an inexpensive cut of meat, and braising makes it tender enough to cut with a fork. The shoulder cut of veal is best for stews. Boned breast of veal is excellent for veal roast, stuffed and rolled before pan-roasting.

Beef is not a favorite with Italians for two reasons: The cow is prized for her milk and the ox for his labor. But although relatively few cattle in Italy are raised for their meat, the country produces some of the best beef in the world. Admired by cattle raisers everywhere are the Chianina beef cattle of Tuscany. Their meat makes the best charcoal-broiled steak in Florence (Bistecca alla Fiorentina) and is also featured on many famous Italian-American restaurant menus. Still, the Italians' most common way of cooking beef, regardless of the cut, is slowly, in pot roasts and stews with wine, herbs, and vegetables.

Italians eat a considerable amount of pork, mostly in the form of sausage and ham. In many northern Italian dishes, pork is barely visible, yet is vital to the flavor.

When an animal is slaughtered in Italy, no part of it goes to waste. Sweetbreads, brains, and liver are often a part of the Italian menu.

Traditionally, lamb is synonymous with Easter and spring in the Italian home. It can provide extremely elegant dishes, such as Agnello alla Fiorentina, leg of lamb seasoned with garlic, herbs, and wine and roasted with vegetables.

Sicilian Piccata

Yield: 4 servings

Piccata is another word for *scaloppini*. *Piccata* comes from *picchiata*, meaning "beaten," since the slices of veal are pounded before cooking.

4 veal scallops, cut in half (about 1 pound total)
Flour
2 eggs, beaten
Fine dry bread crumbs
1/4 cup olive oil
About 2 ounces grated Parmesan cheese
Finely minced parsley
1/4 cup butter
3 garlic cloves, minced

Dust each slice of veal with flour. Dip it into the beaten eggs and then into the bread crumbs, coating it well.

Heat the oil in a heavy skillet over medium-high heat. When the oil is hot, add the veal. Reduce the heat, and fry the veal gently on both sides, until lightly browned.

Place the veal scallops on a hot serving dish, and sprinkle them with Parmesan cheese and parsley. Discard the oil, and add the butter to the same pan. Melt the butter very quickly over high heat. When it begins to foam, remove the skillet from the heat, and add the garlic. Stir well, and return the skillet to the heat for about 3 seconds. Remove the skillet from the heat again, and, with a spoon, coat the veal scallops with the garlic butter. Serve immediately.

Salvatore Bruno
Pinocchio
Paris, France

Scalopine di Vitello alla Toscana

(Veal Scallops from Tuscany)
Yield: 4 to 6 servings

A northern Italian dish found primarily in Tuscany and Emilia-Romagna, where fresh herbs are widely used in cooking.

1 pound veal scallops
1/2 cup all-purpose flour
1/4 cup melted butter
1/4 pound mushrooms, chopped
1 garlic clove, minced
1 shallot, minced
2 fresh sage leaves, minced
6 fresh basil leaves, minced
Pinch fresh thyme leaves, minced
1/3 cup Marsala wine
Salt and pepper to taste
2 tablespoons heavy cream

Dust the veal scallops with flour.

Melt the butter in a heavy skillet. When the butter is hot, add the veal scallops and cook them very briefly on each side. Drain off all the butter and fat from the pan. Add the mushrooms, garlic, shallot, herbs, wine, salt, and pepper. Heat until the wine is reduced. Add the heavy cream, stir, and serve.

Eugenio Massoni
Ristorante Marcello
San Francisco, California

Mignonettes di Vitello alla Regina Vittoria

(Queen Victoria Veal Slices)
Yield: 4 servings

1/4 cup butter
8 thin slices veal
2 cups finely diced assorted cheeses (Fontina, Bel Paese, mozzarella, Parmesan, etc.)
2 ounces prosciutto, chopped
3 tablespoons heavy cream
1/2 cup pâté de foie gras
Salt and pepper to taste
Parmesan cheese

Preheat the oven to 375°F.

Heat the butter in a heavy skillet. Add the veal and briefly saute the veal on both sides. Remove the pan from the heat, and keep the veal warm.

In a saucepan, mix all the cheeses. Melt the mixture over low heat until it is smooth; then stir in the chopped prosciutto and the cream. Heat briefly.

Spread 4 of the veal slices with pâté de foie gras, and lay another veal slice atop each of these. Season with salt and pepper, and pour the melted cheeses over the veal sandwiches. Place the skillet in the oven for 10 minutes, or until the cheese begins to brown. Sprinkle Parmesan cheese over and serve.

Fratelli Zuccarini
Giovanni and Mario Forti Ristorante "G. Ranieri"
Rome, Italy

Veal Siciliano

Yield: 2 servings

An often requested dish at Faustini's, named for the Sicilian Red Corvo wine with which it is made. Mr. Faustini prefers canned tomatoes from the San Marzano region of Italy; they are riper and sweeter than canned American tomatoes.

12 ounces veal scallops
Flour
1/2 cup olive oil
1 medium-size green pepper, julienned
1/2 medium-size Spanish onion, sliced
6 to 8 peeled plum tomatoes (preferably from San Marzano)
12 green olives, pitted
12 black olives, pitted
3/4 cup Red Corvo wine
1/4 teaspoon salt
1 teaspoon garlic powder
1/4 teaspoon freshly ground black pepper
1/2 tablespoon dried oregano
1/2 cup chicken stock

Evenly coat both sides of each veal scallop with flour. Pour 1/4 cup of the oil into a heavy skillet, and fry the veal scallops until they are light brown on both sides. Drain off all the oil, and set the pan aside.

In another skillet, heat the remaining 1/4 cup oil. Add the pepper and onion and saute until the onion is transparent. Drain off the oil, and add the peppers and onions to the skillet containing the veal.

Gently squeeze the plum tomatoes, discarding as much of the juice as possible while keeping the tomatoes whole. Add the tomatoes, olives, wine, and remaining ingredients to the veal. Heat until the liquid bubbles, then simmer over low heat for 10 to 15 minutes, shaking the pan back and forth until the sauce thickens. Serve with Red Corvo wine.

Robert A. Faustini
Ristorante Faustini
East Haven, Connecticut

Veal Scalopine Mamma Chiara

Yield: 4 servings

This recipe originated on the Isle of Capri.

1/4 cup butter
4 slices veal scallops
4 slices Italian smoked ham
1 cup sliced mushrooms
Parsley
2 small zucchini, sliced thin
1/2 pound mozzarella, grated or thinly sliced
Minced garlic
Minced fresh rosemary

Preheat the oven to 400°F.

Melt the butter in a heavy skillet. When the butter is hot, add the veal slices and saute them briefly on both sides. Remove the pan from the heat. Lay on top of each veal slice one slice smoked ham, 1/4 cup of the mushrooms, some zucchini slices, and a sprinkle of parsley; top with 1/4 of the mozzarella. Bake for about 15 minutes, or until the cheese melts. Transfer the veal to hot plates, and sprinkle with a bit of minced garlic and rosemary. Serve with white wine.

Eduardo Napolano
Trattoria aux Trois Continents, Inc.
Montreal, Quebec, Canada

Saltimbocca alla Romana

("Jump in Your Mouth," Roman-Style)
Yield: 6 to 8 servings

This famous Roman dish combines salty prosciutto, veal, and wine. It is a combination so tasty it will "leap into your mouth," which is the literal translation of the name.

2 pounds veal scallops, each about 4 inches
   square
2 tablespoons minced fresh sage or 1 teaspoon
   dried sage
1/8 teaspoon freshly ground black pepper
1/4 pound paper-thin prosciutto slices,
   trimmed to about 4 inches square
3 to 4 tablespoons butter or margarine
1/4 cup dry white wine

Sprinkle one side of each veal slice with some sage and pepper. Top with a slice of prosciutto, and secure the prosciutto with a toothpick.

In a large skillet over moderately high heat, melt the butter. Brown the veal quickly on both sides. Transfer the veal to a heated platter, remove the toothpicks, and keep the platter warm.

Pour the wine into the skillet and heat it. Let the wine boil, uncovered, for 1 to 2 minutes, scraping up any brown bits with a wooden spoon. Pour the sauce over the veal and serve.

Ron Frieborn
Indian Wells, California

Cerino's Veal Parmigiana

Yield: 2 servings

Of all the veal dishes made in Italy, this is the one most commonly served in the United States.

2 eggs
1/2 cup milk
2 (4-ounce) veal scallops (1/4 inch thick)
Salt and pepper to taste
Flour
Dry bread crumbs
1/4 cup oil
2 slices prosciutto
1 tomato, sliced
4 slices mozzarella cheese
Paprika

Preheat the oven to 400°F.

Beat the eggs and milk together.

Season the veal with salt and pepper. Dip the veal scallops into the flour, then into the egg mixture (allowing the excess to drain off), and finally into the bread crumbs; coat the meat well.

In a heavy skillet, heat the oil. Add the veal and brown on both sides. Place the browned veal scallops on a baking sheet. Top each with a slice of prosciutto, 2 slices of tomato, and 2 slices of mozzarella cheese. Sprinkle with paprika, and place the baking sheet in the oven for about 5 minutes. Serve immediately.

Carrie Cerino
Carrie Cerino's Restaurant
North Royalton, Ohio

Veal Luciano

Yield: 4 to 6 servings

The creator of this dish, Luciano Mase, was raised in Pinzolo, Italy, in the northern Italian Alps. His cooking is highly influenced by what he ate as a child. Our meal at Luciano's was most memorable—and filling.

This recipe also works well with pork or chicken in place of veal.

5 chicken livers
2 Italian sausages, skinned and crumbled
1 garlic clove, minced
1 tablespoon minced fresh parsley
2 to 3 tablespoons grated Parmesan cheese
2 egg yolks
3 bacon slices, cut into small pieces
Fresh sage leaves
1 1/2 pounds veal scallops (or pork or chicken), each about 4 inches square
Flour
1/4 cup butter
Salt to taste
1/2 cup dry white wine
1/2 cup chicken stock

Combine the chicken livers, sausage meat, garlic, parsley, Parmesan, and egg yolks, and mix them into a paste. Spread a portion of the mixture on each veal scallop. Tightly roll up the slices and secure them with toothpicks. Put a small piece of bacon and one sage leaf on each toothpick. Dust all the veal rolls with flour.

Melt the butter in a heavy skillet. When the butter is hot, add the veal rolls and brown, turning occasionally. Sprinkle them lightly with salt, add the white wine, and continue cooking slowly until the wine has evaporated. Add the stock and cover the pan. Continue to cook until the veal is tender, approximately 20 minutes.

This dish is delicious with rice or polenta.

Luciano G. Mase
Luciano's Cabin Restaurant
Clinton, Connecticut

Fagottini alla Bruno

(Bruno's Small Bundles)
Yield: 4 servings

The small bundles in this case are veal rolls, stuffed with ham and Parmesan cheese, then pan-fried. The recipe originated in Tuscany; I was served it in Milan.

8 thin slices cooked ham
8 veal scallops
8 oblong pieces Parmesan cheese (preferably Grano Padano)
Flour
1 tablespoon olive oil
2 tablespoons butter
1 tablespoon white wine

Place 1 slice of ham on each slice of veal. In the center of each piece of ham, place 1 piece of Parmesan cheese. Carefully roll up each veal scallop and secure the roll with toothpicks. Dredge each roll in flour.

Combine the olive oil and butter in heavy skillet over low heat. When they are hot, add the veal rolls. Cook the veal rolls, turning them frequently, for about 15 minutes. When they are done, sprinkle them with the white wine. Continue heating until the wine evaporates. Serve at once.

Danilo Spadoni
Trattoria Toscana da Bruno
Milan, Italy

Ossobuco alla Milanese

(Veal Shanks in the Style of Milan)
Yield: 6 servings

This dish originated in Milan, where it was prepared for that city's hierarchy. The veal shanks are stewed very slowly in a mixture of tomatoes, wine, and herbs. The essence of the dish is the bone marrow, which you dig out of the bone with a special little fork that is usually provided. This dish is usually served with a generous helping of rice.

6 (2-inch) slices veal shank, each tied round
  with a string
Flour
1/2 cup butter
1 pound button mushrooms, sliced
1 cup dry white wine
1 1/2 cups peeled Italian tomatoes
Salt and pepper to taste
1/2 cup boiling veal or beef broth
1 tablespoon minced fresh parsley
1 small slice of lemon zest, minced

Dredge the veal shanks in flour.

Put the butter into a heavy casserole that has a tight-fitting lid and is just large enough to contain the veal in 1 layer. Heat the butter; when it foams, add the veal. Sear the veal on both sides, then remove the veal shanks and keep them hot. Add the mushrooms and saute for 2 minutes. Return the veal to the casserole, add the wine, and let it boil. When the wine is reduced, add the tomatoes. Stir gently, adding the salt and pepper. Add the boiling broth, stir a little more, then cover the casserole and reduce the heat. Simmer gently for 2 hours.

Put the meat on a serving dish, pour the pan juices over, and sprinkle with the minced parsley and lemon zest. Serve with risotto or mashed potatoes.

Michele Pavia
George's
Rome, Italy

Veal Bolognese
Yield: 2 servings

4 thin slices baked or boiled ham
2 veal scallops, cut in half
4 slices mozzarella cheese
1/4 cup ricotta cheese
2 eggs
1/2 cup milk
Flour
Dry bread crumbs
1/4 cup vegetable oil
Alfredo Sauce (optional) (see page 29)

Lay a slice of ham on each half-scallop. Pound the ham and veal together. Lay a slice of mozzarella atop each slice of ham. Spread 1 tablespoon of the ricotta cheese over each ham and cheese-covered scallop.

Beat the eggs and milk together. Roll up the scallops, and secure the rolls with toothpicks. Dredge the rolls in flour, dip them in the egg and milk mixture, and cover them with bread crumbs.

Heat the oil in a heavy skillet. Saute the breaded scallop rolls until they are golden brown.

Alfredo Sauce makes an excellent topping for these veal rolls.

Michael Gennaro, Jr.
Gennaro's Ristorante
Charleston, South Carolina

Costolette alla Valdostana

(Veal Chops from Valle d'Aosta)
Yield: 6 servings

Cheese, particularly fontina cheese, is abundant in the mountainous Valle d'Aosta region, where the rich, high-altitude pastures support herds of dairy cows. At any trattoria, you are likely to be served dishes that are enhanced by cheese. These chops are stuffed with fontina cheese, breaded, and pan-fried.

6 veal chops
1/4 pound fontina cheese, thinly sliced
Salt and white pepper to taste
2 1/2 tablespoons all-purpose flour
1 egg, well beaten
1/4 cup fine dry bread crumbs
6 tablespoons butter

Slit each chop horizontally, almost to the bone, to make a pocket. Push slices of fontina cheese into the pockets. Lay the chops flat, press the tops and bottoms together, and seal the edges by beating hard. Lightly sprinkle both sides of the chops with salt and pepper. Dip the chops into flour, then into egg, and finally into bread crumbs; coat them well.

In a skillet, melt the butter. When the butter is hot, add the veal chops. Fry on both sides until they are golden brown, about 10 to 15 minutes. Serve hot.

Louis Cristallo
Brasserie Valdotaine
Aosta, Italy

Osso di Vitello Stracotto

(Braised Veal Chops)
Yield: 4 servings

A tasty meal for guests that does not involve a lot of last-minute work in the kitchen. At Taverna 58, the chops are served on a wooden chopping board with the sauce separate, in a sauceboat.

1/2 cup olive oil
4 veal rib chops, with the bones (about 1 pound total)
Flour
2 to 3 sprigs fresh rosemary
4 garlic cloves, minced
1 cup dry white wine
1 teaspoon whole black peppercorns
Salt to taste

Preheat the oven to 300°F.

Gently heat the oil in a heavy ovenproof pan. Dredge the chops in flour, add them to the pan, and brown them on both sides. Add the rosemary, garlic, and wine, and heat until the wine evaporates. Add the peppercorns, 1 quart water, and a little salt. Stir to mix the ingredients, then transfer the dish to the oven.

Bake, uncovered, for about 2 hours, adding water if necessary. When done, the meat will be a nice brown color, and it will rest in a little sauce. Serve with a wine such as Montepulciano d'Abruzzo.

Giovanni Marrone
Taverna 58
Pescara, Italy

Costata di Manza al Barolo

(Boned Rib of Beef in Barolo Wine)
Yield: 6 to 8 servings

3-pound boned rib of beef
1 onion, quartered
1 carrot, sliced
1 celery rib, roughly chopped
1 bay leaf
Salt
4 to 5 black peppercorns
1 liter Barolo red wine
2 tablespoons chopped lard or butter
1/4 cup butter
1 teaspoon potato flour or cornstarch

Combine the meat, onion, carrot, celery, bay leaf, a little salt, and the peppercorns in a large bowl. Pour the wine over all. Allow the meat to marinate for 24 hours, turning it occasionally.

Remove the meat from the marinade, and carefully pat it dry. Reserve the marinade. With a string, tie the meat into a round.

Strain the marinade into a saucepan, and boil it over fairly high heat until it is reduced by half.

Heat the lard in a pan that is large enough to hold the meat and that has a tight-fitting lid. As the fat begins to melt, add the butter. Stir until the butter is melted. Add the meat, and brown it on all sides. Season the meat with salt and pour the reduced wine over it. Cover the pan, and cook the meat over low heat for about 2 hours, or until it is very tender. (You should be able to eat it with only a fork or, even, a spoon). Transfer the meat to a heated serving dish, and keep it hot.

Skim the fat from the sauce and bring it to a boil again. Mix the potato flour or cornstarch to a thin paste with a little water and stir into the boiling sauce. Cook, stirring constantly, for 5 minutes. Pour a little of the sauce over the meat, and serve the rest separately.

Paolo Donati
Taverna della Rose
Turin, Italy

Filetti al Vermouth

(Beef Filets with Vermouth)
Yield: 4 servings

2 to 3 pounds filet of beef, cut 1-inch thick
1/4 cup butter
1/2 cup sliced green olives
1 teaspoon salt
1/4 teaspoon freshly ground black pepper
1/4 cup dry vermouth
1/4 cup heavy cream

Trim the fat from the filets. Melt the butter in a skillet. When the butter is hot, add the filets and the olives. Cook the filets over high heat for 2 minutes on each side, shaking the pan a few times. Sprinkle the meat with salt and pepper and pour the vermouth and cream over it. Reduce the heat, and cook the filets 2 minutes more on each side for rare meat, or longer if you desire.

Arrange the filets on a hot serving dish and pour the sauce from the pan over them.

"C.C." Gatta
Indian Wells, California

Filetto alla Fiorentina

(Beef Filet from Florence)
Yield: 4 servings

4 tablespoons olive oil
1 carrot, minced
1 onion, minced
1 celery rib, minced
2 garlic cloves, minced
1 to 2 ounces chicken livers, minced
1/2 cup red wine
2 1/2 to 3 pounds beef filet, sliced 1 to 2 inches
  thick
1/4 pound mushrooms, minced
1 cup peeled, seeded, and pureed or chopped
  tomatoes
Salt and pepper to taste
1/2 cup beef stock

Heat 3 tablespoons of the olive oil in a heavy pan. Add the carrot, onion, celery, and garlic, and saute the vegetables until they soften. Add the chicken livers, and cook until they are done. Add the red wine; simmer until the wine has evaporated.

In a heavy pan with a lid, heat the remaining 1 tablespoon olive oil. Brown the beef slices on both sides for a few minutes. Add the wine-simmered livers and vegetables, the mushrooms, tomato puree, salt and pepper, beef stock, and 1/2 cup water. Cover the pan and cook slowly for about 30 minutes. Serve.

Cinali Marino
Ristorante Mamma Gina
Florence, Italy

Olivette della Casa

(House-Special Meat Rolls)
Yield: 6 servings

These are the specialty of the house at Al Pero in Padua, where we feasted on this simple dish.

1/4 cup bread cubes (1/2-inch pieces)
Milk
1 egg, beaten
1 (8-ounce) can plum tomatoes, pureed
1/4 cup fresh bread crumbs
1 1/2 pounds ground beef (not too lean)
3/4 cup grated mozzarella cheese
1/4 cup grated Parmesan cheese
2 tablespoons dried parsley

Preheat the oven to 350°F.

Soak the bread pieces in milk. Drain off the excess milk.

In a large bowl, combine the egg, 1/3 cup of the tomato puree, the bread crumbs, and the bread pieces. Mix in the beef. Mold the mixture into a square or rectangular loaf about 3/4 inch thick.

In a small bowl, combine 1/2 cup of the mozzarella cheese, the Parmesan cheese, and the parsley. Spoon the cheese mixture onto the center of the meat, leaving a 1-inch border of meat all around. Roll up the meat, pressing the edges to seal the roll.

Place the roll seam side down on a baking dish. Bake, uncovered, for about 30 minutes, or until the meat is nearly done. Spoon the remaining tomato puree over the meat roll, and continue baking for a few minutes. Sprinkle the top with the remaining 1/4 cup mozzarella cheese, and bake a little longer, until the cheese melts.

Remove the meat roll from the oven and cut it so the mozzarella filling appears in the center of each round slice. Serve hot.

Salvadego Guglielmo
Al Pero
Padua, Italy

Stracotto al Chianti Classico

(Braised Beef in Chianti)
Yield: 4 servings

A recipe handed down from the famous Medici family. I translated it from a cartoon recipe handwritten in Italian by Sr. Rossi.

A *stracotto* is quite similar and sometimes identical to a *stufato*. Both are meat that is cooked slowly in either wine or tomatoes.

Olive oil
1 onion, minced
2 garlic cloves
1/3 cup pine nuts
1/4 cup blanched almonds
1/3 cup sultana raisins
1 bottle Chianti Clarico wine
2-pound boneless chuck roast
1 carrot, chopped
1 small green pepper, chopped
Salt and black pepper to taste
2 cups beef broth

Preheat the oven to 325°F.

In a saucepan, heat 1 tablespoon olive oil. Add the onion and saute until soft.

In a mortar, pound the garlic, pine nuts, and almonds with a little oil to make a paste. Add the raisins and pound. Add the whole mixture to the pan with the sauteed onion. Stir in the Chianti.

Tie the pot roast with string to hold it together.

In a heavy skillet, heat enough olive oil to just cover the bottom of the pan. When the oil is quite hot, add the meat. Brown it well on all sides, then remove it and set it aside.

In the same pan over moderate heat, saute the carrot and green pepper. Season with salt and pepper.

Combine the roast in a roasting pan with the sauteed vegetables and the beef broth. Cover the pan and place it in the oven. Bake for 2 hours, basting frequently with the wine sauce. When the meat is done, the juices will have turned nearly a caramel color. Serve promptly.

K. Rossi
Giovanni Da Verrazzano
Greve-in-Chianti, Florence, Italy

Todd's Special

Yield: 8 to 10 generous servings

A beef, sausage, and spinach dish served throughout Italy and particularly enjoyed in Turin.

3 cups red wine
2 cups olive oil
3 tablespoons butter
2 medium-size onions, chopped
1 whole garlic bulb, the cloves separated and
  peeled
2 pounds beef (preferably sirloin), diced
Salt and pepper to taste
2 pounds Italian sausages
1 (10-ounce) package frozen chopped spinach
1/3 pound Parmesan cheese, grated
3 (4-ounce) cans button mushrooms, sliced
3 eggs, beaten
2 pounds linguine, cooked (optional)

Heat the wine. Keep warm.

In a heavy deep pan, heat the oil and butter. Add the onions and garlic cloves and saute until they are soft; then add the diced beef. Sprinkle salt and pepper over the meat as it browns. When the meat has browned, stir in the wine.

In another pan, brown the sausages.

While the sausages cook, add the spinach to the beef mixture. Stir frequently as the spinach thaws; continue heating and stirring until it is cooked.

When the sausages are done, slice them 1/4 inch thick. Add the sausage to the beef mixture. Blend in the cheese well, then add the mushrooms. Mix in the eggs just before serving.

Serve Todd's Special over fresh linguine or by itself. A dry red Italian wine is a must with this dish.

Todd Linder
Linderoni's Pasta Deli
Billings, Montana

Fegato Burro Salvia

(Calf's Liver with Sage and Butter)
Yield: 4 servings

A very simple dish which originated in Tuscany, a region known for the simplicity of its cuisine. The secret to success in this dish is to skin the liver carefully and slice it very thin.

12 very thin slices calf's liver, freshly skinned
1/2 pound unsalted butter
12 fresh sage leaves
Salt to taste

Heat a heavy skillet.

In a separate pan, melt the butter and add the sage. Do not let the butter burn.

While the butter melts, sprinkle the liver on both sides with salt. When the skillet is as hot as possible, place the liver slices in it. Turn them after 30 seconds, heat 30 seconds more, and then immediately transfer the liver to a warm platter. Liberally coat the slices with the sage butter.

This dish goes well with boiled fresh spinach and "pearled" potatoes.

Roberto Musetti
Estoril da Luigi e Roberto
London, England

Agnello Scoytadito

(Lamb)
Yield: 2 to 4 servings

An old Roman recipe.

4 tablespoons butter
1 onion, chopped
1/4 pound mushrooms, sliced
1/4 pound tomatoes, peeled and chopped
1 pound lamb filet, cut into 1-inch strips
1 tablespoon paprika
1 garlic clove, crushed (optional)
Salt and pepper to taste
1/4 cup whiskey, heated
1/2 cup light cream
1/2 cup good brown stock
Mashed potatoes
Broiled mushrooms
Parsley
Watercress

Melt 2 tablespoons of the butter in a heavy skillet. Add the onion and saute until it is soft but not brown. Add the mushrooms and tomatoes, and saute for a few minutes. Remove the pan from the heat.

In a separate pan, melt the remaining 2 tablespoons butter. When the butter is hot, add the lamb strips. Saute the lamb until the juices are sealed in. Add the paprika, garlic, and salt and pepper. Continue to cook for 10 minutes, stirring constantly.

Pour the whiskey over the lamb and ignite the liquor with a match. Let the flame subside, then quickly add the cream, brown stock, and sauteed vegetables. Cook for a few minutes more, stirring constantly, until the sauce is well mixed and warmed through.

Serve on a platter inside a border of piped mashed potatoes. Garnish with broiled mushrooms, parsley, and watercress.

Marroli Franaure
Hostario dell' Orso
Rome, Italy

Coniglio con Pinoli

(Rabbit with Pine Nuts)
Yield: 5 servings

1 garlic clove, minced
2 teaspoons minced fresh rosemary
2 teaspoons minced fresh sage
1 teaspoon salt
Pinch freshly ground black pepper
1/4 cup pine nuts
1 rabbit (about 3 pounds)
2 tablespoons olive oil
White wine

Preheat the oven to 200°F.

In a mortar, mix the garlic, rosemary, sage, salt, and pepper; pound in the pine nuts. Press open the rabbit's rib cage, pushing back the ribs. Spread the pine nut mixture all over the cavity. Make slashes in the fore and hind thighs, and fill them with the same mixture. Close the rib cage with toothpicks, and rub the rabbit with the leftover pine nut mixture.

In a heavy ovenproof pan with a lid, heat the olive oil. Brown the rabbit on all sides. Add a little white wine to the pan, cover the pan, and place it in the oven. Bake for about 1 1/2 hours, basting occasionally with white wine, until the rabbit has reached a fine brown-red hue.

Slice the rabbit and serve. Baked vegetables are a good accompaniment.

Gianni Brunelli
Osteria Le Logge
Siena, Italy

Coniglio al Fiori di Finocchio

(Rabbit Baked with Flowers of Fennel)
Yield: 4 servings

In this country, flowers of the wild fennel are not commercially available, but you can easily find the seeds in the spice shelves of the supermarket to grind with a mortar and pestle.

At Locanda dell'Amorosa in Siena, this dish is garnished with pureed potatoes mixed with parsley, butter, a touch of nutmeg, and grated Parmesan cheese.

Brown Sauce

2 pounds veal bones
2 carrots, peeled
1/4 cup chopped onion
1/2 pound fresh tomatoes
2 tablespoons tomato paste
3 liters white wine
Salt to taste

Rabbit

Saddle of rabbit (from the base of the neck to the top of the thigh)
Salt and pepper to taste
1/2 ounce flowers of fennel or 3 tablespoons freshly ground fennel seeds
2 to 4 tablespoons butter

In a large pot, combine the veal bones, carrots, onion, tomatoes, tomato paste, and 3 quarts of water. Cook over low heat for 7 hours, occasionally skimming off the fat and adding water as necessary to keep the bones covered. Strain the sauce. Over low heat, reduce the sauce to half its original volume.

In another saucepan, boil the wine to evaporate the alcohol. Reduce the wine by half, and add it to the brown sauce. Cook the sauce for several minutes and season it with salt.

Preheat the oven to 325°F.

Sprinkle the rabbit with salt, pepper, and fennel flowers or seeds. In an ovenproof pan, heat the butter. Saute the saddle of rabbit over medium heat, taking care not to burn the butter.

Transfer the pan to the oven and bake for 25 minutes. Remove the rabbit, and drain off the fat, taking care not to remove the fennel flowers. Bone the saddle. Slice the meat, and place it on a heated platter. Cover it with the hot sauce and serve.

Marchese Carolo Citterio
Locanda dell'Amorosa
Sinalunga, Siena, Italy

Coniglio alla Reggiana

(Rabbit in the Style of Reggio Emilia)
Yield: 4 to 6 servings

7 tablespoons oil
5 tablespoons red wine vinegar
Fresh sage leaves, minced
Fresh rosemary leaves, minced
Juniper berries
Salt and pepper to taste
2 1/4-pound to 4 1/2-pound rabbit

In an enamel or stainless steel pot, combine the oil, vinegar, juniper berries, sage, rosemary, salt, and pepper. Mix well.

Wash the rabbit first in a bowl of hot water, then in a bowl of cool water. Cut it into 8 pieces, and put all the pieces in the pot with the marinade. Turn the rabbit pieces to coat them. Cover and let the rabbit marinate for 1 hour, turning the pieces every 10 minutes.

Set the pot over low heat and cook, covered, for at least 1 hour. Serve the rabbit immediately, or let it cool and refrigerate it for later reheating.

Ivan Lusetti
Cooperativa Reggiana Ristorante Virgiliano
Mantua, Italy

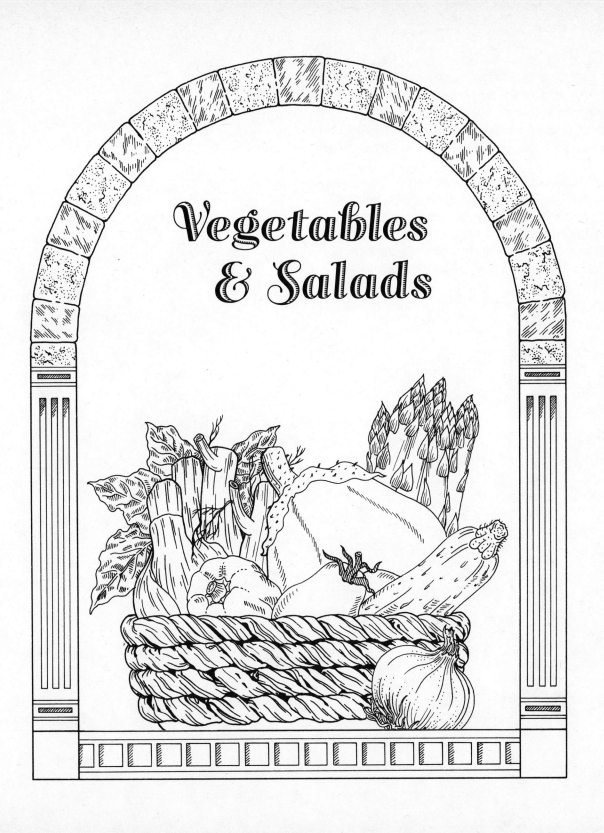

Vegetables
& Salads

egetables and salads are given considerable importance and careful treatment in Italian cuisine. Most often they are served as separate courses after the meat.

Eggplants are one of the most popular vegetables in Italy, particularly in the South, where Eggplant Parmigiana was invented. Indeed, you will encounter eggplant prepared in countless ways if you eat your way through the South.

Other vegetables a traveler is likely to encounter in Italy include beans, lentils, asparagus, artichokes, celery, fennel, bell peppers, spinach, potatoes, salad greens, and, of course, tomatoes.

Eggplant Parmigiana

Yield: 4 servings

The classic Sicilian eggplant dish.

1/2 cup (or more) dry bread crumbs
Salt, pepper, and dried oregano to taste
1 egg (or more), beaten
1 or 2 tablespoons milk
1/4 cup olive oil
1 large or 2 small eggplants, peeled and cut into
   slices no more than 1/4 inch thick
2 cups Marinara Sauce (page 42)
1/2 pound mozzarella cheese
Parmesan cheese

Season the bread crumbs with salt, pepper, and oregano.

In a bowl, mix 1 egg with 1 tablespoon milk.

Preheat the oven to 350°F.

In a skillet, heat the olive oil over high heat. When the oil is very hot, reduce the heat to medium-high. Dip the eggplant slices into the milk-egg mixture, then into the seasoned bread crumbs. Fry the slices, a few at a time, for 3 to 4 minutes on each side, or until they are lightly browned. Reserve the fried slices on a paper-towel-lined platter until all are done. You may need additional seasoned bread crumbs and milk-egg mixture depending on the number of eggplant slices you have.

In a shallow casserole, spread several tablespoons of the tomato sauce. Cover the sauce with a layer of eggplant slices, brush the eggplant with tomato sauce, and sprinkle mozzarella cheese over the sauce. Add another layer of eggplant, more sauce, and more cheese, and continue layering the ingredients until you've used all the eggplant. The top layer should be cheese. Place the casserole in the oven and bake for 30 minutes, or until the cheese is bubbly and lightly browned.

Offer Parmesan cheese at the table for sprinkling.

Alfred B. Carangelo
Santa Barbara, California

Eggplant Sorrentino

Yield: 6 servings

Olive oil or vegetable oil
6 thick slices eggplant (from the center of a large eggplant)
Flour
1 egg, beaten
6 thin slices mozzarella cheese
6 thin slices cooked ham
18 ounces ricotta cheese
Salt and pepper
Paprika
Minced fresh parsley
Grated Parmesan cheese
Marinara Sauce (see page 42)
Grated mozzarella cheese

Preheat the oven to 450°F.

Heat enough oil to come 1 inch up the side of a skillet.

Lightly flour the eggplant slices, then dip them into the egg. When the oil is hot, fry the eggplant slices just until they are golden. Place them on paper towels to drain off the excess oil.

When the eggplant has cooled, place atop each slice 1 slice mozzarella cheese, 1 slice cooked ham, 3 ounces (a little more than 1/3 cup) ricotta cheese, a pinch each of salt, pepper, paprika, and parsley, and some grated Parmesan cheese. Then roll each slice with its topping and secure the roll with toothpicks.

Spread some Marinara Sauce on the bottom of a casserole dish and arrange the eggplant rolls on top of sauce. Top them with more Marinara Sauce, and sprinkle mozzarella cheese over. Bake for 10 to 15 minutes, until the cheese is melted and bubbly. Serve.

Angelo Verrico and Tony Musci
D'Angela Trattoria
Laguna Hills, California

Eggplant della Mamma

Yield: 4 servings

Mamma Montesano's interesting version of stuffed eggplant.

2 medium-size eggplants
1/2 cup olive oil
1/2 pound sweet Italian sausage, diced
1 onion, minced
3 garlic cloves, minced
1/2 cup white wine
6 fresh basil leaves, minced
Pinch ground red pepper
3 tablespoons chopped fresh parsley
1 cup fresh bread crumbs
Salt and pepper to taste
1 1/2 cups grated fontina or mozzarella cheese

Preheat the oven to 350°F.

Cut the eggplants in half lengthwise, and scoop out most of the insides, leaving 1/2 inch of flesh all the way around. Dice the scooped-out eggplant.

In a skillet, heat the olive oil. When the oil is hot, add the diced eggplant and saute for 2 minutes over medium heat. Add the sausage, and saute until it is cooked, about 4 to 5 minutes. Add the onion, garlic, white wine, basil, red pepper, parsley, and bread crumbs. Blend together well, and add the salt and pepper. Stir in the cheese and stuff the mixture into the eggplant shells.

Place the stuffed eggplant halves on a baking pan. Bake for 30 minutes or until the stuffing is golden brown on top.

Mamma Montesano
Montesano Ristorante Italiano
Houston, Texas

Torta Pasqualina

(Easter Pie)
Yield: 6 servings

This classic is rich not only with flavor but also with meaning: the eggs symbolize fertility, the spinach symbolizes the yearly renewal of the earth, and the 33 layers of dough represent the years of Christ's life. The fillings of these tortas may vary from cook to cook, but you will find them throughout Italy at Easter time.

8 cups all-purpose flour
5 tablespoons olive oil
1 teaspoon salt
2 pounds fresh spinach
Olive oil
1/2 onion, minced
1 pound ricotta cheese
1 cup milk
Salt to taste
1/4 cup butter
6 eggs
Freshly ground black pepper to taste
Pinch dried marjoram
1/4 cup grated Parmesan cheese

Mix the flour, 5 tablespoons oil, and salt, and gradually add enough water to make a stiff dough that leaves the sides of the bowl cleanly. Knead the dough. Divide it into 10 balls of equal size (originally it was divided into 33 pieces, one for each year of Christ's life). Put the dough balls on a lightly floured pastry board, cover them with a damp cloth, and leave them for 15 minutes.

Meanwhile, wash the spinach, and cook it in as little water as possible until it is soft. Drain well.

In a pan, heat 1 tablespoon olive oil. Add the onion and saute until it is soft but not brown.

Drain the spinach, chop it finely, and add it to the onion. Mix and cook the onion and the spinach for a few minutes longer, then set the pan aside.

In a bowl, mix the ricotta cheese with the milk and a pinch of salt. Set the bowl aside.

Preheat the oven to 400°F.

Brush a deep, wide pie dish with olive oil. Roll 1 dough ball into a wafer-thin sheet a little larger in diameter than the dish; keep the rest of the balls under the damp cloth. Line the pie dish with the dough disk, brush it lightly with oil, and trim away the excess dough. Roll out another dough disk, lay it over the first, and continue layering oil and dough until 6 disks are in the pie dish. Spread the sixth disk with the onion and spinach mixture; spread the ricotta cheese over. Hollow out 6 evenly spaced wells in the filling, and drop a sliver of the butter and 1 egg into each. Sprinkle with salt, pepper, marjoram, and Parmesan cheese. Roll out the last 4 dough balls, and layer them with oil brushed between. Prick the top layer with a fork, brush it generously with oil and trim off the excess dough.

Bake for about 40 minutes, or until the pie is golden brown. Serve hot or cooled.

Pasquini Diva
Nannina
Imperia, Italy

Insalata di Pasta con Frutta di Mare

(Pasta Salad with Seafood)
Yield: 6 servings

1 pound fusilli
1/4 Spanish onion, cut into chunks
1/2 lemon
1 celery rib
2 garlic cloves
3 bay leaves
12 medium shrimp, peeled and deveined
1/2 pound sea scallops
1/2 pound red snapper, cut into chunks
1/2 pound baby clams
1/2 pound cooked crabmeat
1 teaspoon chopped garlic
1 teaspoon chopped fresh parsley
1 teaspoon chopped fresh basil leaves
1 sweet red pepper, chopped
1 green pepper, chopped
3/4 cup virgin olive oil
Salt and pepper to taste

Cook the fusilli in plenty of boiling salted water for 7 to 8 minutes, or until it is tender but still firm. Drain the fusilli, rinse it with cold water, and drain it again.

Bring to a boil 1 gallon salted water with the onion, lemon, celery, garlic cloves, and bay leaves; boil for 3 minutes. Then add all the seafood, except the crabmeat, and boil for 2 minutes. Drain and let cool at room temperature.

Place the pasta, boiled seafood, and crabmeat in a large bowl, and mix together. Add the chopped garlic, parsley, basil, red and green peppers, and the olive oil. Add salt and pepper, mix thoroughly, and serve.

Luigi Bosco
Bosco's Ristorante Italiano
Atlanta, Georgia

Insalata Verde

(Green Salad)
Yield: 6 to 8 servings

1 medium-size head escarole
1 medium-size head chicory
1 medium-size head romaine lettuce
1/4 cup olive oil
1 tablespoon red wine vinegar
Salt and pepper to taste
1 cup garlic croutons

Separate the leaves from the heads of greens, and wash the leaves well. Shake them dry, and wrap them lightly in several paper towels; chill the wrapped greens thoroughly.

At serving time, break the leaves into medium-size pieces and drop them into a chilled salad bowl.

Whisk together the oil and vinegar. Pour the dressing over the greens, and toss a few times. Add salt and pepper if needed. Add the croutons, and toss again, gently, just enough to distribute the croutons evenly and to coat all the leaves with dressing.

Anna Dolceacqua Carangelo
Santa Barbara, California

Italian Spinach Salad

Yield: 4 servings

From the Isle of Capri.

1 pound fresh young spinach
6 bacon slices
1/4 cup olive oil
1 tablespoon red wine vinegar or lemon juice
Salt and pepper to taste
1 small garlic clove, crushed
6 to 8 raw asparagus spears
2 ounces mozzarella cheese, grated
A few black olives

Rinse the spinach by immersing it in plenty of water. Cut off the stems and spin the leaves dry.

Cut the bacon into small strips, put the strips in a skillet, and fry them to the desired crispness. Drain the bacon strips on paper towels, and let them cool.

Combine the olive oil, vinegar or lemon juice, salt and pepper, and garlic. Mix the dressing well.

In a salad bowl, toss the spinach with the bacon and dressing. Add the grated mozzarella cheese, olives, and asparagus spears. Toss again lightly, and serve.

Eduardo Napolano
Trattoria aux Trois Continents, Inc.
Montreal, Quebec, Canada

Insalata di Radicchio

(Red Chicory Salad)
Yield: 6 servings

Radicchio has recently become very popular in the United States. In Italy, there are 3 different varieties of this lovely vegetable. The varieties with the long leaves have the best flavor; the variety with the cabbage-like head, most commonly found in the United States, lacks the delicate flavor of the other radicchios. Still, this is a delicious salad with any variety of radicchio, and it can be made with other greens, including dandelion greens, with excellent results.

2 pounds radicchio
12 slices bacon (about 1/2 pound)
2 garlic cloves, crushed
1/3 cup red wine vinegar
1 egg, beaten
Salt and pepper to taste

Separate the leaves of the radicchio and wash them thoroughly by immersing them in plenty of water. Drain the greens, and dry them between paper towels. Tear them coarsely into a serving bowl.

Cut the bacon into 1/2-inch strips and put them in a skillet with the garlic. Set the pan over moderate heat, and cook the bacon thoroughly without letting it become crisp. Remove and discard the garlic. Slowly (to avoid splattering) stir the vinegar into the bacon and the rendered fat. Let the mixture heat through to blend the flavors, and then remove the pan from heat. Let the dressing cool; then pour it over the greens. Blend in the beaten egg, and season the salad with salt and pepper. Serve immediately.

Maria Grazia Benevento Dolceacqua
Salerno, Italy

Grande Crisantemo

(Grand Chrysanthemum)
Yield: 8 servings

This dish celebrates fresh mozzarella; the original kind, made from buffalo's milk, is best. Supermarket mozzarella is no substitute.

1/2 cup mayonnaise
3 tablespoons whipped cream
1 pound fresh mozzarella, sliced
5 medium-size pears
Juice of 1 lemon
5 to 6 lettuce leaves
6 heads Belgian endive, the leaves separated
1 small head radicchio
1/2 cup walnut pieces

In a small bowl, mix the mayonnaise and cream; chill the mixture.

Place the mozzarella in a colander to drain.

Peel and slice 4 of the pears into wedges. Drop the wedges into a medium-size bowl, add the lemon juice, and cover the pears with water (this acidulated water will prevent the pears from discoloring).

Line a round or oval serving dish with the lettuce. Cut the mozzarella slices into strips. In a petal-like pattern on top of the lettuce, alternate endive leaves, pear slices, and mozzarella strips; leave room in the center of the plate for a round of radicchio leaves and, in the very middle, a whole peeled pear. Arrange a second layer of endive leaves, mozzarella strips, and pear slices around the whole pear, overlapping the radicchio and the first endive-pear-mozzarella layer. Continue layering the endive leaves, pear slices, and the mozzarella strips, in imitation of a chrysanthemum, until all are used.

Sprinkle the chrysanthemum with the walnut pieces. Serve the mayonnaise-cream sauce on the side.

Bruno Creglia
Giordano Restaurant
New York, New York

Countryman's Salad
Yield: 4 servings

4 not-too-ripe Bartlett pears, peeled and quartered
3 to 4 ounces provolone cheese, cut into sticks
1 bottle sparkling wine
4 basil leaves
4 mint leaves
Olive oil
White pepper
1 head curly endive

Put the pears in a bowl, along with the provolone cheese and half the wine. Cover the bowl, and let the flavors blend for about 1 hour.

Arrange the endive on 4 salad plates. With a slotted spoon, transfer the pears and cheese to the salad plates and arrange on top of the endive. Dress each salad with olive oil, a basil leaf, a mint leaf, white pepper, and a little of the wine in which the pears and cheese marinated. Serve, passing the remaining half bottle of wine to drink at the table.

Maria Sentuti
"G.B."
Rome, Italy

Pizza
&
Foccacia

FLOUR

When most of us Americans think of Italian food, we immediately think of pizza (or "pizza pie" as it was originally introduced in the northeastern United States). For many of us, pizza offered our first taste of Italian cooking.

The word *pizza* literally means "to flatten"; pizza is a flat leavened bread. In the Bible, in the Book of Kings, Elijah baked a "cake" on coals "and went in the strength of that meat for 40 days and 40 nights." The Italians called Elijah's cake *focaccia* from the Latin *focus*, meaning "hearth." Long after Elijah baked his cake, Pliny the Elder mixed "the foam of the beer" (yeast) into flour. Evidence that Romans baked risen round loaves has been found in the ruins of Pompeii and Herculaneum.

There are many different versions of focaccie in Italy, though all start with flour, salt, yeast, and water. Often fresh herbs are kneaded into the dough; some contain cheese. A favorite is Focaccia alla Genovese, which is served doused with the local olive oil. Focaccia is often served as a snack and makes a great accompaniment to soups and salads.

Pizza, as we know it today, is the invention of the Neapolitans, who began improving their circle of crust with lard, oil, herbs, and, when it was available, cheese. Not until Columbus brought the tomato to Italy from the New World was *pizza al pomidoro* born—an affordable treat in the household of an Italian peasant. In the sixteenth century, the Tavern of Cerriglio in Spaccanapoli, Italy, was the first tavern anywhere to serve a tomato-and-mozzarella pizza as we know it in the United States.

The first pizzeria in America was opened in the first decade of this century, in Manhattan. It specialized in Pizza Margherita, the tomato-mozzarella-basil pizza said to have been admired by Queen Margherita because it bore the colors of the Italian flag. Pizza Margherita became known here as Pizza Neapolitan Style, and its fame soon spread throughout the country, along with Pizza Sicilian, New York Pizza, Chicago-style Pizza, and California-style Pizza.

A genuine Neapolitan pizza is very different from what is produced in most American pizza shops. It differs in the methods of baking, in the taste of the dough, and in the taste of the tomato topping.

Genuine Neapolitan pizza is baked not in a pan but on a hot brick or stone surface. Because this method lets excess oil escape, a Neapolitan pizza never tastes greasy or fried. The crust is crisp on the outside and firm throughout, faintly sour but not yeasty tasting, and never spongy or rubbery. Except for the raised edges, the crust has a uniform thickness of not more than 3/8 inch.

The tomato topping for a real Neapolitan pizza is not a sweetened sauce, but simply tomatoes; ideally, they are fully ripe so they can go into the oven raw (the watery tomatoes sold in markets must be scalded with a little olive oil before they can go on a pizza). If you cannot find good fresh plum tomatoes, substitute a high-quality imported Italian brand of the San Marzano variety.

Popular Pizzas

There are as many variations on the basic pizza recipe as there are bakers. Here is a listing of some of the pizza variations you may encounter at pizzerias in Italy and abroad.

Alle Cozze (*with Mussels*). Add 1 pound shelled mussels during the last 5 to 10 minutes of cooking.

Margherita of della Regina (*of the Queen*). Substitute fresh basil for oregano, and add sliced or diced mozzarella cheese (no garlic). This pizza is said to have been made for Queen Margherita because it bears the colors of the Italian flag—red, white, and green.

Alla Romana (*Roman-Style*). Add anchovies (fileted or coarsely chopped) and a pinch of pepper. Finish with sliced mozzarella and a sprinkling of grated Parmesan cheese.

Alla Siciliana (*Sicilian-Style*). Add chopped onions and anchovies. Finish with shredded caciocavallo or provolone cheese.

Alla Ligure (*Ligurian-Style*). Season with rosemary instead of oregano and add a handful of pitted black olives.

Antica alla Frattese (*Ancient from Fratta*), or **Bianca** (*White*). Omit the tomatoes; this pizza predates their adoption in Italy. Top the pizza with just grated cheese, oil, and a pinch of pepper. Provolone, Pecorino Romano, or caciocavallo cheese is used. Mozzarella may be added.

All'Ortolana (*Kitchen Garden-Style*). Omit the tomatoes and substitute roasted and peeled red, yellow, and green peppers, cut into strips. Add a handful of green olives.

Alla Siracusana (*Syracuse-Style*). Omit the fresh tomatoes. Top with fried eggplant, mozzarella slices, oregano, peppers, green olives, and a few spoonfuls of tomato sauce.

All'Amalfitana (*Amalfi-Style*). Omit the tomatoes. Top with 1/2 pound raw small sardines (their heads removed) dressed with a mixture of olive oil, salt, pepper, and minced garlic.

Congliocchi (*with the Eyes*). Top with tomato slices, oil, anchovies, grated Parmesan cheese, and pepper. Bake for 15 minutes. Break 4 eggs on top of the pizza and bake for 5 more minutes. Add salt and continue baking until the eggs are done, 5 to 8 minutes.

Della Luna (*of the Moon*). Spread oil on the dough with your fingers; add nothing else. Bake for 20 minutes, then top with 1/4 cup pesto.

Quattro Stagioni (*Four Seasons*). Score uncooked, flattened pizza dough into 4 sections with a knife. Place a different condiment in each section, as follows. First section: pitted black olives with chopped anchovies and oil. Second section: pickled artichokes in oil. Third section: sauteed mushrooms. Fourth section: raw mussels or clams tossed in olive oil (minced garlic is added during the last 5 minutes of baking). Other topping variations might be: tomato slices and diced mozzarella; prosciutto strips and diced mozzarella; chopped onions, Gruyère cheese, and ham; sauteed onions and zucchini; eggplant and oregano.

Also choose for pizza toppings: greens, fennel, cardoons, caviar, pancetta, sausage, salami, tripe, figs, chicken livers, pineapple, spaghetti, hearts of palm, tuna, snails, eels, squid, smoked salmon, smoked herring, shrimp, prawns, seaweed, oysters, asparagus, broccoli.

The Perfect Pizza Oven

In 1830, the first pizzeria appeared in Naples. It had a brick-lined oven, fired by wood. The wood was soon replaced by Vesuvian lava, which was able to retain the high temperature needed to make the best pizzas.

A conventional home oven can be transformed into something very much like a baker's oven by lining it with quarry tiles or a baking stone. The tiles or stone must be preheated for at least 30 minutes ahead of baking. If you can't find baking stones or other pizza-making equipment or ingredients locally, write to the suppliers listed in the back of this book.

Rising to the Occasion: About Yeast

Egyptians fermented bread dough six thousand years ago. At first the dough was thought to be spoiled and was thrown away. The Hebrews refused to eat this leavened bread. But the Egyptians learned to take advantage of the fermentation by keeping a small piece of yeasty dough as a "starter" for fresh dough. If you take the Roman *moretum* or the Tuscan *schiacciata* (both flat, unleavened circles of dough) and let it rise before baking, you have pizza as it was first made.

Throwing the Pizza

One final note on the mystery of pizza making concerns the debate over why the *pizzaiola* (pizza maker) throws the circle of dough into the air, sometimes executing twirls and loop-the-loops and catching it without its losing shape, folding, or tearing. Some say this is to allow more air to reach the rising dough, or to test its elasticity before adding the topping and baking it. But all agree that accomplished pizza makers enjoy doing acrobatics with the dough, as much as their customers enjoy the show.

Authentic Neapolitan Pizza Crust

Yield: One 10- to 11-inch Pizza Crust

1 1/2 cups semolina or hard wheat flour
  (substitute all-purpose flour if necessary)
1 teaspoon salt
1/2 ounce compressed yeast or 1 1/2 teaspoons
  (1/2 package) active dry yeast, dissolved in
  1/2 cup lukewarm water
1 tablespoon olive oil

Pour the flour onto a work surface, shape it into a mound, and make a shallow well in the center. Place the salt, dissolved yeast, and olive oil in the well, and draw the sides of the dough with your hands until all the ingredients are well blended and form a ball of dough. Knead the dough for about 8 minutes. (You can instead blend the ingredients in a food processor and knead by hand for 5 minutes.)

Put the kneaded dough in a lightly floured bowl. Fold a damp dish towel in half and lay it over the bowl. Place the bowl in a warm, draft-free place, such as an unlit oven with a gas pilot. The dough is ready to use when it has doubled in volume. If you are not ready to bake the pizza then, however, no harm will be done if you leave the dough in the bowl for an extra hour or two.

When the dough is ready for the toppings, set the oven at 450°F and begin heating the pizza stone or tiles. The stone or tiles should heat for at least 30 minutes.

Roll out the pizza dough into a disk about 10 or 11 inches in diameter and about 1/4 inch thick. Turn the dough over from time to time as you roll it to keep it from shrinking back. Try not to roll past the edges. As you reach the desired diameter, use your fingertips to push some of the dough from the center toward the edge, making the edge at least twice as thick as the rest of the crust. Place the dough on a lightly floured wooden paddle or sheet of cardboard (a light sprinkling of cornmeal also helps to prevent sticking and adds flavor to the bottom of the crust).

When you are ready to bake the pizza, spread the toppings evenly over the dough so the pizza will not become soggy. Slide the pizza from the paddle onto the hot stone or tiles. Bake the pizza for 15 to 20 minutes, until the edge has turned golden with a few specks of brown. Serve hot.

Anna Benevento
Dal Delicato
Naples, Italy

Pizza alla Napolitana

(Neapolitan Pizza)
Yield: 10-inch to 11-inch pizza

Neapolitan pizza is topped with garlic, tomatoes, and olive oil; no cheese is added. Though today considered the most traditional pizza, this is a descendent of the older oil and garlic pizza. At its best with good tomatoes and fresh, sweet garlic, Neapolitan pizza has no rivals.

Pizza dough (page 107)
5 tablespoons olive oil
1 1/2 pounds fresh plum tomatoes, peeled, seeded, and chopped; or 2 cups canned Italian plum tomatoes, thoroughly drained, seeded, and chopped
Salt
4 medium-size garlic cloves, sliced very thin
2 tablespoons dried oregano
6 to 12 anchovy fillets

Prepare the pizza dough according to the recipe directions.

Preheat the oven to 450°F and begin heating a pizza stone or tiles. The stone or tiles should heat for at least 30 minutes.

Heat 3 tablespoons of the olive oil in a pan. When the oil is hot, add the tomatoes. Cook them briefly over high heat, stirring, to evaporate excess moisture.

Roll out the dough for a 10-inch to 11-inch pizza and place it on a wooden paddle or sheet of cardboard. Top the dough with the tomatoes, a sprinkling of salt, the garlic, the oregano, and the anchovies; then pour the remaining 2 tablespoons olive oil in a thin stream evenly over the pizza. Slide the pizza onto the hot stone or tiles, and bake for 15 to 20 minutes, until the puffed rim of the crust turns golden. Serve hot.

Anna Benevento
Dal Delicato
Naples, Italy

Focaccia
Yield: 6 servings

Like a thick pizza, focaccia has a smoother, more bread-like texture. In Puglia, this would be called a *puddica*.

Pinch salt
4 1/2 cups all-purpose flour
2/3 ounce compressed yeast or 1 tablespoon (1 package) active dry yeast, dissolved in 1/2 cup warm water

Mix the salt with the flour; add the dissolved yeast and about 1 1/2 cups more water to make a soft but firm dough. Knead until the dough is smooth and elastic. Let it rise for at least 30 minutes, until it has doubled in bulk.

Preheat the oven to 400°F. Roll out the dough at least 1 1/2 inches thick, and place in greased pan. Bake for 30 to 45 minutes, until golden. Let it cool before cutting and serving. It is very good with cheese, ham, salami and so on.

Variation

Add to the dough or top the dough with any one or more of the following: rosemary, sage, garlic, tomatoes, cheeses, sausage, onions, ciccioli (cracklings), hard-boiled eggs, or prosciutto. You can also substitute white wine for water in the dough, Puglian style.

Richard Proto
West Haven, Connecticut

Pizza Margherita

Yield: 10-inch to 11-inch pizza

This pizza, in the red, white, and green colors of the Italian flag, was made for Queen Margherita in 1889. The anchovies traditionally used in Neapolitan-style pizzas are omitted and mozzarella is added.

For Pizza alla Romana, use both mozzarella *and* anchovies.

Pizza dough (page 107)
6 ounces whole-milk mozzarella
5 tablespoons olive oil
1 pound fresh ripe plum tomatoes, peeled, drained, and cut into strips
1 teaspoon salt or to taste
1 tablespoon dried oregano
1 tablespoon grated Parmesan cheese

Prepare the pizza dough according to the recipe directions.

Unless you can find buffalo mozzarella, prepare the mozzarella cheese as follows: Shred or grate it into a bowl. Add 3 tablespoons olive oil, mix thoroughly, and let the cheese steep for at least 1 hour. Fresh buffalo mozzarella should be simply grated.

In a medium-size saucepan, heat the remaining 2 tablespoons olive oil. Add the tomatoes with the salt and cook, covered, for 2 to 3 minutes. When the tomatoes have softened a bit, remove the lid and cook for about 7 minutes more, stirring frequently. Transfer the tomatoes to a strainer, and let the excess liquid drain into a bowl for 5 minutes. Then mash and strain the tomatoes. Set them aside to cool.

Set the oven at 450°F and begin heating a pizza stone or tiles. The stone or tile should heat for at least 30 minutes.

Roll out the dough for a 10-inch to 11-inch pizza, and place it on a wooden paddle or sheet of cardboard. Spread the tomatoes evenly over the dough, then sprinkle on the salt, the mozzarella, the oregano, and the Parmesan cheese. Slide the pizza onto the preheated baking stone or tiles and bake for 15 to 20 minutes, until the puffed rim of the dough is golden. Serve hot.

Anna Benevento
Dal Delicato
Naples, Italy

Sfincione

(Pizza)
Yield: 6 servings

In Palermo, street vendors and bake shops sell sfincione instead of pizza. The recipe here is for an open sfincione, which is much like a pizza. Sfincione di San Vito is closer to a pie than a pizza: its rich filling of sausage and ricotta is stuffed between two layers of bread dough.

Dough

1/3 cup olive oil
Juice of 1 lemon
Salt and pepper to taste
1/4 cup grated Pecorino Romano or
  caciocavallo cheese
3 1/2 cups all-purpose flour
2/3 ounce compressed yeast or 1 tablespoon (1
  package) active dry yeast dissolved in 1/2 cup
  warm water

Topping

1/3 plus 1/4 cup olive oil
1 large onion, chopped
3 to 4 tomatoes, peeled, seeded, and chopped
1/4 cup chopped fresh parsley
3/4 cup diced Pecorino Romano or caciocavallo
  cheese
6 anchovy fillets, washed and cut into pieces
2 tablespoons dry bread crumbs

To make the dough, warm 1/3 cup olive oil, and add the lemon juice, salt, pepper, and cheese. Work this mixture into the flour, then add the dissolved yeast. You should get a soft but firm dough. Knead it well.

Dust a large bowl with a little flour. Add the dough. Make 2 crossed incisions in the top. Cover the dough with a cloth, and put the bowl in a warm place. Let the dough rise until it is doubled in bulk, about 2 hours.

While the dough rises, prepare the topping. Heat 1/3 cup olive oil in a pan and add the onion and tomatoes. Saute for a few minutes, then add the parsley, cheese, and 2/3 of the anchovy pieces. Cook gently over low heat for 10 to 15 minutes. Set the pan aside.

When the dough has doubled in bulk, briefly knead it again. Spread it on a greased round baking pan. Let it rise for another 30 minutes in a warm place.

Preheat the oven to 400°F.

With your finger, make indentations in the top of the dough, and spread half the topping over it. Bake the sfincione for 30 minutes. While the sfincione bakes, heat 1/4 cup olive oil with the dry bread crumbs in a frying pan. Take the sfincione out of the oven, and cover it with the rest of the topping. Garnish it with the remaining chopped anchovy, cover the top with the fried bread crumbs, and moisten with a little fresh olive oil. Bake the sfincione for another 10 minutes to bind the topping together and serve.

Richard Proto
West Haven, Connecticut

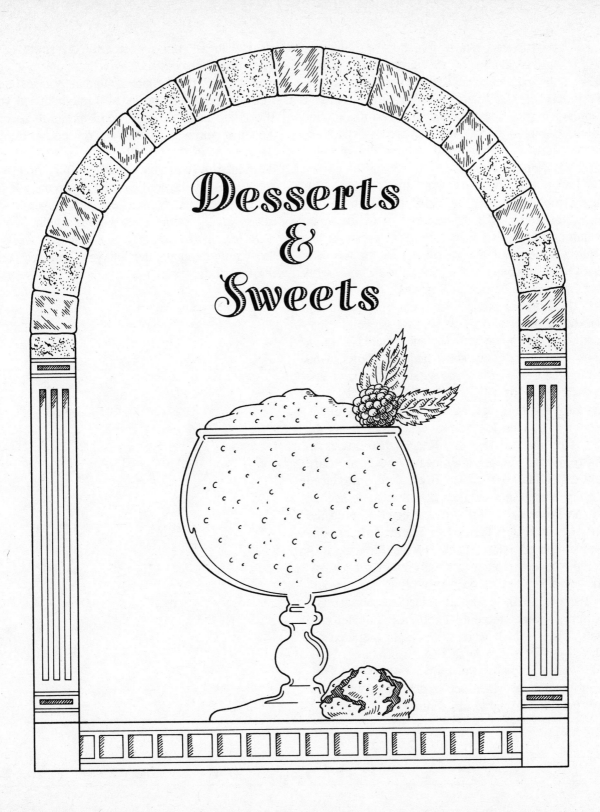

Desserts
&
Sweets

Few travelers return from Italy without rapturous reports of the pastries and gelato they consumed throughout the country. They talk of afternoons spent at cafes, drinking espresso and eating the most wonderful almond-filled, lemon-scented, rum-flavored, chocolate-coated pastries. They speak of cannoli, biscotti, crespelles, and torta.

Italian ices and ice creams are considered by many to be the best in the world. It was an Italian, Giovanni Bosio, who in the last half of the nineteenth century was the first to sell ice cream in the United States. But the art of making frozen desserts began four hundred years before Christ, with the Chinese, Indians, and Persians.

The Romans brought ice from the mountains, packed in straw and wool, because Emperor Nero liked his fruit juice ice-cold and filtered through snow. The Arabians, and later the Turks, who conquered the Middle East, acquired the art of ice-making from the Persians in 1191, when Richard the Lion-Hearted met the Turkish Sultan Soliman. And the Italians learned to make ices from the Arabs in the Middle Ages. Renaissance noblemen enjoyed fruit sherbet after heavy meals at court, and an Italian cook named Bountalenti introduced the sherbets at the wedding of Catherine de Medici to the French dauphin. An Italian cook prepared sherbet for King Charles I of England almost one hundred years later. Thanks to the Sicilian, Procopio, the common man finally could partake of the sherbets when he opened the first "ice parlour" in Paris in 1670. It was an immediate success and within six years, more than 250 Parisian cafes sold Italian ices, which were still sorbets prepared according to the Arab-Persian-Chinese recipe of ice-fruit-water. Finally, the Italian owner of a Parisian ice parlour created ice cream, or gelato, in the last half of the eighteenth century.

Gelato is sold by vendors on street corners throughout Europe, and even in some favored areas of the United States. Italian pastries can be found in bakeries and cafes throughout the world. If you are lucky enough to be invited to an Italian wedding, you will have an opportunity to sample a wide range of the best Italian sweets. Italian wedding cake is like none other. Sinfully rich, moist, spongy cake is layered with pastry creme and laced with fruit preserves and liqueur, then topped with roses made from melt-in-your-mouth frosting. Here is a listing of some of the many sweets you are likely to encounter on your culinary travels through Italy.

Ices and Ice Cream

Gelato. Flavored ice cream.

Granita. A frozen slush of fruit juice or coffee and sugar.

Spumoni. Ice cream bombe (many flavors, colors, textures).

Tortoni. Rum-flavored ice cream macaroon treat served in paper cups.

Pastries

Baba Rum. Rum-soaked sponge-cake filled with pastry cream and a dab of fruit.

Cannoli alla Siciliana. Sicilian fried pastry tubes filled with sweetened ricotta cheese.

Pasticca. Small sweet-dough pies filled with vanilla or chocolate cream, with rum-soaked bottoms.

Spolietelle. Special occasion torte.

Other Desserts

Biscotti all'Anise, Anisette. Anisette-flavored biscuit, good for dipping.

Budino di Ricotta. Ricotta pudding.

Cassata Gelata. Ice cream cake.

Cassata di Ricotta. Ricotta cheesecake.

Ciambella Milanese alla Caffe. Milanese coffeecake.

Crespelle. Italian crepes, served warm with orange sauce.

Fiche Ripieni. Stuffed figs.

Panettone. Fruit-bread, a Christmas special.

Pan di Spagna. Sponge cake.

Struffoli alla Napoletana. Neapolitan honeyballs.

Tartine alla Crema. Little cream tarts.

Torta alla Zabaglione. Custard cake with Marsala wine.

Torta di Mele alla Mantova. Apple cake, Mantua-style.

Zabaglione. Custard with Marsala wine.

Zuccotto. Fancy, dome-shaped, layered dessert with sponge cake, liqueur-laced chocolate, and fruit fillings.

Zuppa Inglese. Italian trifle.

Gelato alla Vaniglia

(Vanilla Ice Cream)
Yield: 2 quarts

It is not necessary to have an ice cream maker to produce this wonderful treat.

6 egg yolks
2 cups whole milk
2 cups heavy cream
1 cup sugar
1 teaspoon vanilla extract

Beat the egg yolks until foamy.

Combine the milk, cream, and sugar in the top of a double boiler. Heat the mixture until small bubbles form around the side of the pan. Add a small amount of the cream mixture to the egg yolks, then stir the yolks into the cream in the top of the double boiler. Cook the custard over simmering water, stirring constantly, until it thickens enough to lightly coat a metal spoon. Stir in the vanilla. Strain the custard; let it cool thoroughly.

Freeze the custard in an ice cream maker according to the manufacturer's directions. If you have no ice cream maker, proceed as follows.

Pour the custard into two deep metal freezer trays and cover the trays with foil. Freeze the custard until it is firm, but not hard.

Chill the bowl and beater of an electric mixer. Empty the freezer trays into the mixing bowl; beat the custard at high speed until it has doubled in volume. Return it to the trays and freeze until it is firm, but not hard.

Break up the custard, beat it again, and freeze it until it is firm but not hard.

Beat the frozen custard a third time, then put it into a bowl and cover it. Freeze the gelato until it is firm again, about 2 hours.

Store the gelato in the freezer until you are ready to serve it.

Richard Cicchi
Santa Barbara, California

Gelato al Caffe

(Coffee Ice Cream)
Yield: 1 quart

This is a very simple recipe; if you have an ice cream maker, it takes only 35 minutes to prepare.

3 to 4 ounces instant coffee powder
1 1/4 cups milk, heated
6 egg yolks
1/2 cup sugar
3/4 cup heavy cream

Add the instant coffee to the hot milk, and stir until the coffee dissolves.

In a bowl, beat the egg yolks and sugar. Stir in the hot coffee mixture and blend thoroughly. Let the mixture cool to room temperature, about 20 minutes; then stir in the cream.

Freeze the mixture in an ice cream maker according to the manufacturer's directions, or in a freezer tray, beating the mixture several times as it freezes (see preceding recipe).

Store the gelato in the freezer until you are ready to serve it.

Giolitti Nazzareno
Giolitti
Rome, Italy

Zabaglione

(Custard with Marsala Wine)
Yield: 1 to 2 servings

According to legend, this famous sweet was invented by accident, when the chef to Carlo Emanuele I of Savoy accidentally added some fortified sweet wine to an egg custard. An immediate success, the dish was dedicated to the patron saint of pastry makers, San Giovanni Baylon, hence the name. Zabaglione is said to have great restorative powers, and it is customarily served to newlyweds as an aphrodisiac.

3 yolks of large eggs (or 4 yolks of medium-size eggs)
3 tablespoons sugar
1 cup dry Marsala wine

Heat water in the bottom of a double boiler.

Place the egg yolks in a bowl and add the sugar. Stir with a wooden spoon, always in the same direction, until the sugar is completely dissolved and the mixture lightens in color. Add the Marsala slowly, then transfer the egg mixture to the top of double boiler. Heat over boiling water, stirring constantly, and always in the same direction, until the mixture thickens and sticks to the wooden spoon (4 to 5 minutes). Do not allow to boil. When the mixture has thickened, remove the top pan of the double boiler, and keep stirring for another 2 to 3 minutes to cool the zabaglione. Cover the zabaglione with lightly buttered waxed paper, and let it cool for 1 hour at room temperature; then refrigerate until you are ready to serve it.

Serve the zabaglione in goblets or cups.

Variation

For a creamier zabaglione, whip 1 cup heavy cream with 2 tablespoons sugar and fold into the cooled custard.

David J. Holt
Italia
Seattle, Washington

Granita di Limone

(Lemon Ice)
Yield: 4 servings

One of many Italian fruit ices. Another traditional favorite is coffee-flavored ice.

1 cup sugar
Juice and grated zest of 6 large lemons (about 1 cup of juice and about 1 tablespoon grated rind)

Combine the sugar and 2 cups water in a saucepan. Boil gently for 5 minutes. Cool to room temperature, then stir in the lemon juice and zest.

Freeze the granita in an ice cream maker according to the manufacturer's directions, or in a freezer tray, beating the mixture several times as it freezes (see page 114).

Store the granita in the freezer until you are ready to serve it.

"C.C." Gatta
Indian Wells, California

Cassata all'Italiana

(Italian Dessert)
Yield: 8 servings

Donatello's scrumptious frozen version of the famous Italian cake.

1/3 cup raisins
1/2 cup dry Marsala wine
1/2 cup sugar
2 egg whites
3/4 cup heavy cream, whipped
1/2 cup mixed diced candied fruit
1/2 cup toasted hazelnuts, husked and sliced
3 tablespoons chopped blanched pistachios
1 pound fresh strawberries, hulled
Sugar
Mint sprigs

In a small bowl, soak the raisins in the Marsala for 1 hour. Drain well and set aside.

Heat the sugar with 1/2 cup water in a small, heavy saucepan over low heat, swirling the pan occasionally, until the sugar dissolves. Increase the heat and boil the syrup until a candy thermometer reads 234°F to 240°F (the soft-ball stage).

While the syrup boils, beat the egg whites in an electric mixer until soft peaks form. Slowly pour the hot syrup down the side of the mixer bowl, and beat until the syrup is incorporated and the whites are thick and cool. Gently fold in the whipped cream, candied fruit, hazelnuts, pistachios, and raisins. Spoon the mixture into a 9-inch by 5-inch loaf pan, pressing down to eliminate air bubbles. Smooth the top, cover the cassata with plastic wrap, and freeze for at least 3 hours.

Puree the strawberries in a food processor or blender; strain out the seeds. Add sugar to taste. Run a sharp knife around the cassata. Wrap a hot towel around the pan, and invert the cassata onto a platter. To serve, spoon the strawberry sauce onto plates, and top with slices of cassata. Garnish with mint.

Donatello Ristorante
San Francisco, California

Granita di Mandarino

(Tangerine Ice)
Yield: 4 servings

Juice of 10 tangerines
3/4 cup sugar
Juice of 1 lemon
1/2 cup liqueur (maraschino, kirsch, or Strega)
1 tangerine, peeled and sectioned

Combine the tangerine juice, sugar, lemon juice, and 1/2 cup water in a saucepan. Cook the mixture until it thickens, about 5 minutes. Remove the pan from the heat and let the mixture cool.

Add the liqueur to the cooled juice mixture, and beat with a whip until the liqueur is absorbed. Freeze the mixture in an ice cream maker, according to the manufacturer's directions, or in a freezer tray, beating the mixture several times as it freezes (see page 114).

Serve the granita in goblets; garnish with sections of tangerines.

Marisa Sentuti
"G.B."
Rome, Italy

Semifreddo di Torrone

(Semifrozen Torrone Candies)
Yield: 8 servings

Semifrozen desserts are enjoying a great popularity in American restaurants. Torrone, which forms the basis for this dish, is a fancy nougat candy. It is sold in both hard and soft varieties in Italian markets, some supermarkets, and specialty stores.

3 eggs, separated, at room temperature
1/2 cup sugar
2 3/4 cups heavy cream
2 tablespoons dark rum
1 tablespoon vanilla extract
4 ounces bittersweet chocolate, finely chopped
3 ounces hard torrone, crushed into rice-size pieces
1 1/2 tablespoons powdered sugar
4 teaspoons unsweetened cocoa powder
Chocolate curls

Line a 5-inch by 10-inch loaf pan with plastic wrap, allowing the edges to overhang.

Whisk the egg yolks and sugar in a bowl until the mixture is thick and pale.

Beat 1 1/4 cups of the cream until soft peaks form.

Beat the egg whites until they are stiff but not dry.

Fold the whipped cream, egg whites, rum, and vanilla into the yolk mixture.

Combine the chopped chocolate and torrone in a small bowl. Sprinkle 1/3 of this mixture into the prepared pan. Top with 1/3 of the cream mixture, pressing firmly. Repeat this process 2 more times with the remaining chocolate mixture and the cream. Fold the plastic wrap over the top of the pan, and freeze the dessert for at least 3 hours and up to 1 week.

Unmold the dessert onto a platter. Let it soften for 30 minutes in the refrigerator.

Sift together the powdered sugar and cocoa. Beat the remaining 1 1/2 cups cream until soft peaks form, and fold the cream into the cocoa mixture. Beat the cocoa cream until stiff peaks form.

Spread a thin layer of the cocoa cream over the dessert, covering it completely. Spoon the remaining cream into a pastry bag fitted with a large star tip. Pipe the cream decoratively along the edges and around the base of the dessert. Garnish with chocolate curls and serve.

Britta Cane
Cathedral City, California

Blueberry Tortoni

Yield: 8 servings

Cousin Anna acquired this recipe years ago from Mamma Leone's famous Italian restaurant near the Broadway theaters in Manhattan.

1/2 cup sugar
3 egg yolks
2/3 cup almond paste
3 tablespoons pineapple juice or light cream
Dash salt
1 1/2 cups heavy cream, whipped
1 cup fresh blueberries, rinsed and drained, or
  1 cup frozen unsweetened blueberries
Grated almonds

Combine the sugar and 1/4 cup water in a saucepan, and bring the mixture to a boil. Boil until a candy thermometer registers 240°F.

While the syrup boils, beat the egg yolks until they are thick and lemon colored. Gradually beat the hot syrup into the yolks; continue beating until the mixture is very thick. Gradually beat in the almond paste, pineapple juice, and salt. Fold in the whipped cream, then the blueberries.

Spoon the mixture into 4-ounce souffle cups. Decorate the top of each serving with a few blueberries and grated almonds. Place the cups in the freezer, and freeze until the tortoni are firm. When they are frozen hard, wrap them in plastic freezer wrap to prevent crystallizing. Serve frozen.

Anna Arpaia Tropeano
Mamma Leone's
New York City, New York

Pere Cotte con Crema e Cioccolato

(Pears Stuffed with Chocolate and Whipped Cream)

Yield: 12 servings

12 ripe bosc pears
2/3 cup lemon juice
6 cups white wine
Zest of 1/2 lemon
4 whole cloves
2 cups sugar
1 1/3 cups orange juice
Whipped cream
Chopped nuts
Hot chocolate sauce

Peel each pear, but leave the stem attached. Slice off the bottom of the pear so it will stand up straight. Remove the core and line the hollow with aluminum foil. Stand the pears upright in a saucepan. Pour in the lemon juice, white wine, and enough water to cover the fruit. Add the lemon zest, cloves, sugar, and orange juice. Simmer, covered, for about 20 minutes, or until the pears are tender.

Remove the pears from the saucepan and place them on a serving dish. Cover them with foil and set aside to cool.

Remove the lemon zest and cloves from the syrup, and cook the syrup over low heat for about 1 1/2 hours to reduce it. Let the syrup cool.

After the pears have cooled, remove their foil lining. Lay each pear on its side on a small serving dish. Fold the chopped nuts into the whipped cream, and gently spoon the mixture into the hollow of each pear. Pour a little syrup over the pear, and decorate it with the hot chocolate sauce. Serve.

Victor Mari Alonso
La Tosca
Dallas, Texas

Spuma di Cioccolata

(Chocolate Mousse)
Yield: 6 servings

8 ounces semisweet chocolate, cut into small
  pieces
3 eggs
1 cup heavy cream
1/4 cup orange-flavored liqueur or rum
  (optional)
Whipped cream
Grated semisweet chocolate

Melt the chocolate over very low heat or in a mircrowave. Set aside to cool slightly.

Beat the eggs in a medium-size bowl until they are foamy. Set aside.

Beat the heavy cream in a large bowl until stiff peaks form. Gradually beat the eggs into the cooled chocolate. Blend in the orange liqueur or rum, if desired; do not overbeat the mixture. Fold the chocolate mixture into the whipped cream until thoroughly combined.

Spoon the mousse into individual dessert glasses, and decorate with whipped cream and grated chocolate. Refrigerate the glasses overnight. Serve the mousse chilled.

Frances Arpaia Raccio
Clinton, Connecticut

Fiche Ripiene

(Stuffed Figs)
Yield: 4 servings

As an antipasto served with prosciutto, stuffed figs are very popular all over Italy. But this recipe is less common; here figs are stuffed with a cheese filling, to be served at the end of the meal, as a dessert.

4 ripe even-sized figs
Yolk of 1 large egg
1/4 cup sugar
8 ounces (1 cup) ricotta cheese
1 to 2 tablespoons brandy
4 shelled whole almonds

Cut the figs lengthwise down the middle, but do not cut all the way through. Cut each half lengthwise down the middle, but again, don't separate the pieces completely. Open out each fig in quarters, and place it on a serving plate.

In a bowl, combine the egg yolk, sugar, and cheese; beat together until the mixture is light. Add the brandy, and fold it lightly into the cheese mixture. Spoon some of the mixture into the center of each fig, and top each dessert with an almond. Serve.

Maria Grazia Benevento Dolceacqua
Salerno, Italy

Fiche al Cioccolato

(Stuffed Figs in Chocolate)
Yield: 1 1/2 pounds

1 pound large dried figs
1 cup toasted almonds
3/4 cup diced candied citrus peel
2 cloves, pounded or ground
3/4 cup unsweetened cocoa powder
3/4 cup powdered sugar

Preheat the oven to 350°F.

Trim any long stems from the figs, and cut the figs lengthwise, just through the center, not all the way through. Stuff each fig with an almond, a few pieces of candied peel, and a pinch of clove. Gently press the fig shut.

Arrange the stuffed figs on a baking sheet. Bake for 15 minutes, or until the figs darken slightly.

While the figs bake, sift the cocoa and sugar together into a shallow dish. Remove the figs from the oven, let them cool enough to handle, and roll them in the cocoa mixture. Serve them when they have cooled completely, or store them in an airtight container.

Eduardo Capelli
Normanni
Praia a Mare, Cosenza, Italy

Cerino's Ricotta Cheesecake

Yield: 10-inch cheesecake

1 pound ricotta cheese
1 pound cream cheese
2 cups sour cream
1 1/2 cups sugar
4 eggs
3 tablespoons all-purpose flour
3 tablespoons cornstarch
3 tablespoons lemon juice
1 teaspoon vanilla extract
1/2 cup melted butter
Graham cracker crumbs

Mix together the cheeses, sour cream, and sugar. Add the eggs, 1 at a time; do not overmix. Stir in the flour, cornstarch, lemon juice, and vanilla extract. Fold in the melted butter.

Butter a 10-inch springform baking pan and dust it well with graham cracker crumbs to form the crust. Pour in the cheese mixture. Place the cheesecake in a cold oven, then set the temperature at 325°F. Bake for 1 hour, then turn off the oven. Remove the cake from the oven 2 hours later, and remove the side of the springform pan. Slide the cake off the bottom of the springform pan and onto a plate. Serve cooled.

Carrie Cerino
Carrie Cerino's Ristorante
North Royalton, Ohio

Ricotta Rice Pie

Yield: 3 (10-inch) pies

The recipe for this traditional Easter treat was passed on to Cousin Marie from her mother-in-law years ago. Marie and her sisters, Anna and Frances, are great Italian-American cooks.

Crust

3 tablespoons butter or margarine
4 cups all-purpose flour
1 cup sugar
4 teaspoons baking powder
4 eggs
4 teaspoons vanilla extract
1 teaspoon lemon extract, orange extract, or orange juice

Filling

1 dozen eggs
2 cups plus 2 tablespoons sugar
1 quart milk, warmed
Juice and grated zest of 1 orange
Juice and grated zest of 1/2 lemon
2 pounds ricotta cheese
2 cups cooked white rice
Nutmeg (optional)

Cut the butter into the flour with a fork or pastry blender. Blend in the sugar and baking powder. Beat the eggs, one at a time, and add them to the flour mixture, mixing after each egg is incorporated. Mix in the extracts. Form the dough into a ball. Knead in a little water or orange juice if necessary. Divide the dough into thirds. Form each piece into a ball; roll out each ball on a floured surface. Lay the dough in three 10-inch pie pans; trim away the excess and pinch the edges.

Preheat the oven to 350°F.

For the filling, beat 6 egg whites with 2 tablespoons sugar until the whites are stiff. Set them aside.

Beat 6 whole eggs with the remaining 6 yolks and 2 cups sugar. Add the orange juice and zest and the lemon juice and zest to the warm milk. Add the milk and juice mixture to the whole egg and sugar mixture. Stir in the ricotta cheese and cooked rice. Beat all the ingredients together, then fold in the egg whites until the mixture is smooth. Dust the crust with a little flour, then pour in the filling. Sprinkle the pie with nutmeg, if you like.

Put aluminum foil around the edge of each pie and place the pies in the oven. Bake for about 1 hour, or until the filling has set. Check the pies after 45 minutes; if they are brown, reduce the heat to 300°F and continue baking. Serve warm or cooled.

Marie Arpaia Negri
Manchester, Connecticut

Italian Rum Cake

Yield: 8 servings

Cake

6 eggs, at room temperature
1 cup sugar
1 cup instant flour
1/2 cup unsalted butter or margarine, melted
  and cooled
1 teaspoon vanilla extract
1/4 cup rum

Rum Butter Frosting

1/2 cup butter, softened
1 pound powdered sugar, sifted
1 egg, well beaten
1 teaspoon vanilla extract
2 tablespoons dark rum

Preheat the oven to 350°F.

With an electric mixer, beat the eggs at high speed until they are thick and lemon-colored. With the beater still running at high speed, add the sugar gradually, 1 tablespoon at a time. When you have added all the sugar, beat the mixture for 10 minutes, or until it has tripled in volume. Gradually, fold in the flour with a wooden spoon. (Instant flour makes for a smooth, fine-grained cake that is easy to handle.) Pour the melted butter slowly into the batter, leaving the milky residue behind in the pan. Fold the butter into the batter. Fold in the vanilla extract.

Grease the bottoms (only) of two 9-inch layer-cake pans. Line the bottoms with foil, and grease the foil. Pour the batter into the pans, and spread it evenly. Bake the cake for 25 to 30 minutes, or until it feels springy to the touch. Cool the cake in the pans for 10 minutes. With a sharp knife, cut the sides of the cake away from the pan. Remove the cake from the pans, remove the foil, and let the cake cool on racks. Sprinkle each layer with rum.

To make the frosting, cream the butter until it is soft and fluffy. Gradually beat in some of the sugar. Beat in the egg, vanilla, and rum. Beat in the remaining sugar gradually, until the frosting has a good spreading consistency.

When the cake has cooled completely, spread frosting over 1 layer, and put the second layer on top. Spread frosting over the second layer, then over the side of the cake. Refrigerate the cake to harden the frosting; this makes it easier to cut neat, thin slices.

"C.C." Gata
Indian Wells, California

Castagnioli

(Fried Dough)
Yield: 8 to 10 servings

2 teaspoons vegetable oil
6 eggs, well beaten
3 tablespoons whiskey or rum
Zest of 1 lemon
1 tablespoon sugar
About 2 1/2 cups all-purpose flour
Vegetable oil

Add the 2 teaspoons oil to the beaten eggs and beat the eggs again. Add the rest of ingredients, using just enough flour to hold the dough together.

Heat enough vegetable oil in a frying pan to pan-fry or deep-fry the castagnioli. Drop in large spoonfuls of the dough. Fry the castagnioli until they are golden brown; if you are pan-frying, turn them once. Remove the castagnioli with a slotted spoon and drain them on paper towels. They are a delicious sweet treat when served with honey.

Mary Jeffery
Santa Barbara, California

Sfinge di San Guiseppe

(St. Joseph's Cream Puffs)
Yield: 8 servings

Filling

1 cup ricotta cheese
2 tablespoons chopped semisweet chocolate
1 teaspoon grated orange zest
1/3 cup powdered sugar
1/2 cup heavy cream, whipped
1 teaspoon almond extract

Puffs

1/2 cup butter or margarine
1 cup all-purpose flour
1/4 teaspoon salt
4 eggs
1 teaspoon grated orange zest
8 maraschino cherries
Candied orange peel

For the filling, combine the ricotta cheese, chocolate, orange zest, and powdered sugar. Blend well. Fold in the whipped cream and almond extract. Chill well.

Preheat the oven to 375°F.

For the puffs, combine 1 cup water and the butter in a deep saucepan. Bring to a boil and cook until the butter melts. Quickly stir in the flour and salt. Beat until the dough forms a ball in the center of the pan. Remove the pan from the heat and let it stand for 5 minutes. Add the eggs 1 at a time, beating thoroughly after each addition. Beat in the orange zest. The mixture should be very stiff.

Drop spoonfuls of the mixture onto a buttered baking sheet. Bake the puffs for 20 minutes, or until they are firm and crusty. Prick them with a fork to release steam, and leave them in the oven for another 5 minutes. Remove them from the oven and let them cool.

Cut off the tops of the puffs, and fill them with the cheese filling. Decorate them with maraschino cherries and strips of candied orange peel, and serve.

Maria Grazia Benevento Dolceacqua
Salerno, Italy

Crema Pasticcera

(Pastry Cream)
Yield: 2 cups

This custard forms the basis of many Italian desserts.

4 tablespoons sugar
1 1/3 cups light cream
2 egg yolks
2 whole eggs
2 teaspoons cornstarch
1/8 teaspoon salt
1/4 teaspoon vanilla extract
1/4 teaspoon finely grated lemon zest

In a saucepan over low heat, dissolve 2 tablespoons of the sugar in the cream.

In a mixing bowl, beat together the egg yolks, whole eggs, cornstarch, salt, and the remaining 2 tablespoons sugar. Vigorously beat in the scalded cream, and heat the mixture (without letting it boil) for a few minutes, until the cream thickens. Remove the pan from the heat and stir in the vanilla extract and lemon zest. Let the mixture cool, then chill it. Crema Pasticcera may be kept under refrigeration for 2 to 3 days; do not freeze it.

Variations

For Chocolate Crema Pasticcera, dissolve 2 to 4 ounces semisweet chocolate into the cream as you heat it. For Almond Crema Pasticcera, substitute almond extract for the vanilla extract.

Maria Grazia Benevento Dolceacqua
Salerno, Italy

Pasta Folle

(Filled Pastry)
Yield: 6 servings

A traditional Venetian dessert.

Pastry
1/2 cup butter
2 2/3 cups all-purpose flour
3 whole eggs
2 egg yolks
1 teaspoon vanilla extract
Zest of 1 orange

Filling
1/4 pound spinach, finely chopped
1/2 cup plus 2 tablespoons ricotta cheese
4 eggs
1/2 cup plus 2 tablespoons sugar
Juice of 1 orange
1/4 cup rum

Topping
3 egg whites
1 cup powdered sugar
1 cup chopped almonds
Juice of 1 lemon

To make the pastry, cut the butter into the flour. Slowly stir in the eggs, one at a time, then the yolks, mixing thoroughly. Stir in the vanilla extract and orange rind. On a lightly floured surface, knead the dough briefly until it becomes a smooth mass. Roll out the dough, and line a 9-inch cake pan with it. Trim away the excess dough.

Preheat the oven to 350°F.

To make the filling, cook the spinach and drain it thoroughly. Mix it with the ricotta cheese.

In a separate bowl, beat the eggs with the sugar until light and lemon-colored. Add the orange juice and rum. Combine this mixture with the spinach and ricotta cheese.

To make the topping, beat the egg whites until they are stiff but not dry. Slowly beat in the powdered sugar, 1 tablespoon at a time. Fold in the chopped nuts and lemon juice.

Spread the filling in the pastry-lined pan. Spread the topping over the filling. Place the pie in the hot oven and bake for about 40 minutes. Serve hot.

Franco Zanotto
Il Casino
Wellington, New Zealand

Sicilian Cassata

Yield: 6 servings

This is a homespun and delicious version of a most famous Sicilian sweet.

1 1/2 pounds very fresh ricotta cheese
2/3 to 1 cup sugar
7 tablespoons rum
10 ounces candied lemon peel
3 1/2 ounces unsweetened chocolate, finely chopped
1 pound sponge cake, sliced, or ladyfingers

Using a large bowl and a wooden spoon, cream the ricotta until it is very smooth. Add the sugar, 1 tablespoon of the rum, the candied peel, and the chocolate.

Sprinkle 5 tablespoons of the rum over the sponge cake slices.

Line the bottom and side of a springform pan or souffle dish with parchment paper, and brush the paper with the remaining 1 tablespoon rum. Then line the bottom and side of the pan with sponge cake slices. Fill the middle with the ricotta mixture. Refrigerate the cassata for at least 3 hours, and serve.

Enzo Cortese
Mulino Trattoria
East Sydney, Sydney, Australia

Cannoli alla Siciliana

(Sicilian Pastry Tubes)
Yield: 10 pastries

These Sicilian sweets are readily available in bakeries throughout the United States. They are fried pastry tubes filled with sweetened ricotta.

Filling
1 1/2 cups ricotta cheese
1/4 cup chopped candied fruit
3 tablespoons chopped pistachio nuts or
  almonds
2 to 3 tablespoons chopped semisweet chocolate
3 tablespoons sugar
1/4 teaspoon almond extract

Pastry
1 cup all-purpose flour, sifted
2/3 cup sugar
1/4 teaspoon salt
1/4 cup Marsala wine
Vegetable oil
Powdered sugar

Combine the ricotta cheese, candied fruit, nuts, 2 tablespoons of the chocolate, the sugar, and almond extract. Mix well. Chill. To make the pastry, sift together the flour, sugar, and salt. Stir in the wine. Knead the dough on a floured surface until it is firm and elastic. Add another drop or two of wine, if necessary, but do not allow the dough to become sticky. Place the dough in a lightly floured bowl, cover the bowl with a damp towel, and let it stand for 2 hours.

Roll out the dough on a lightly floured surface to a rectangle 22 1/2 inches by 9 inches; the dough should be 1/8-inch thick. Cut the dough into ten 4 1/2-inch squares. Wrap each square diagonally around a cannoli tube or a clean, unpainted piece of broomstick 6 inches long. Moisten the points that will overlap with a drop of water, and press firmly to seal.

In a large, deep pan, heat vegetable oil to deep-fry the cannoli. Fry them, 3 or 4 at a time, until they are golden brown. Drain them on paper towels for about 30 seconds. Using tongs, carefully slide the forms out of the cannoli. Let the cannoli cool.

Just before serving, fill the cannoli with the chilled ricotta mixture. If you like, garnish the ends with more chocolate, and dust the cannoli tubes with powdered sugar.

Maria Grazia Benevento Dolceacqua
Salerno, Italy

Bocconotti

(Little Mouthfuls)
Yield: 2 to 4 dozen tarts

Jam or custard-filled pastries from Naples.

4 cups all-purpose flour
3 tablespoons sugar
2 to 3 tablespoons vegetable oil
Blackberry or quince jam, or plain or chocolate
  Crema Pasticcera (pastry cream, page 123)
1 egg yolk, beaten

Preheat the oven to 425°F.
Combine the flour and sugar. Mix in the oil and enough water to make a soft dough. On a floured work surface, roll the pastry out thin, and cut out disks 2 or 3 inches in diameter. Place a dab of jam or Crema Pasticcera in the center of each disk. Fold the disk in half, and press the edges firmly together to seal them. Lay the bocconotti on a baking pan, and brush with the egg yolk.

Bake for about 20 minutes; check after 15 minutes, and every 5 minutes thereafter. When done, they will be golden brown. Serve cooled.

Richard Cicchi
Santa Barbara, California

Nepitelle

(Little Tarts)
Yield: 24 tarts

These delectable little tarts are filled with dried fruit and grated chocolate.

Marsala Pastry

2 cups all-purpose flour
1/4 cup sugar
Pinch salt
1/2 cup plus 1 tablespoon butter, well-chilled and cubed
3 tablespoons sweet Marsala wine
2 teaspoons grated lemon zest
1 egg, beaten

Fruit Filling

1/4 cup sweet Marsala wine
1/2 cup raisins
1/3 cup minced dried figs (about 1 1/2 ounces)
3 tablespoons sugar
1 1/2 ounces bittersweet chocolate, grated
1/4 teaspoon ground cinnamon
Pinch salt

To make the pastry, sift the flour, sugar, and salt into a large bowl. Cut in the butter until the mixture resembles coarse meal. Make a well in the center. Add the Marsala, lemon zest, and egg to the well and mix these ingredients with a fork until they are well blended.

Continue mixing, gradually drawing the flour from the inner edge of the well, until all the flour is incorporated. Gather the dough into a ball and wrap it in plastic film. Chill for at least 30 minutes, and up to 2 days.

Butter twenty-four 2-inch tartlet pans. Roll the dough out on a lightly floured surface to a thickness of 1/16 inch. Using a floured cutter or drinking glass, cut out 3-inch-diameter rounds. Fit the rounds into the prepared pans, trim the edges, and refrigerate the pastry shells.

To make the filling, heat the Marsala in a small heavy saucepan. Remove the pan from the heat, add the raisins, and leave them to plump for about 30 minutes. Stir in the figs, sugar, chocolate, cinnamon, and salt. (The filling can be prepared up to 1 week ahead and refrigerated.)

Preheat the oven to 400°F.

Spoon 1 tablespoon of the filling into each pastry shell. Bake until the pastry is lightly browned, 15 to 20 minutes. Cool the tartlets on a rack, then remove them from their pans. Sprinkle them with powdered sugar. Serve the tartlets immediately, or store them at room temperature for up to 1 day.

Britta Cane
Cathedral City, California

126

Struffoli

Yield: 8 servings

These traditional honey-coated Christmas sweets are often piled into a pyramid as a centerpiece for the holiday table; the struffoli are broken off and eaten at the end of the meal.

2 1/4 cups all-purpose flour, sifted
3 tablespoons grated orange zest
1 tablespoon grated lemon zest
1/4 teaspoon salt
3 tablespoons butter, at room temperature
3 eggs, at room temperature, beaten
1/2 teaspoon vanilla extract
Vegetable oil
3/4 cup honey
1 tablespoon sugar
1 cup mixed candied fruit
Additional candied fruit (optional)

Combine the flour, 1 tablespoon of the orange zest, the lemon zest, and the salt on a work surface. Cut in the butter. Mound the mixture and make a well in the center. Add the eggs and vanilla to the well. Mixing with a fork, gradually draw the flour mixture from the inner edge of the well into the center. Mix until the flour is completely incorporated. Knead the dough until it is smooth, about 5 minutes, adding more flour if necessary to prevent sticking. Cover the dough loosely. Let it stand for 1 hour at room temperature.

Break off walnut-size pieces of the dough. With your palms, roll each piece out on a work surface to a pencil-thin strip 14 to 15 inches long. Cut each dough strip into 1/4-inch pieces.

Heat vegetable oil to deep-fry the struffoli. Gently place a few pieces of the dough in the hot oil; do not crowd them. Fry the struffoli, a few at a time, until they are golden brown, 45 to 60 seconds. Remove them with a slotted spoon and drain them on paper towels.

Butter a large plate. Heat the honey and sugar in a large, heavy saucepan over medium heat until the mixture is clear, about 5 minutes. Add the remaining 2 tablespoons orange zest, the struffoli and the candied fruit. Transfer the honey-coated struffoli and candied fruit to the buttered plate, and let them cool slightly, 5 to 7 minutes. Moisten your hands with cold water and shape the struffoli into a pyramid. Decorate the pyramid with additional candied fruit, if desired. The struffoli will keep for 1 day; cover and store the pyramid at room temperature if it is not to be eaten within a few hours.

Roger Smith/Laura Noel
Palm Springs, California

Germinus

(Sardinian Macaroons)
Yield: About 1 pound

4 egg whites
3/4 pound powdered sugar
3/4 pound peeled and slivered almonds
Juice of 1 lemon

Preheat the oven to 325°F.

Beat the egg whites until stiff peaks form. Fold in the sugar together with the almonds and lemon juice. Cover a baking pan with parchment paper, and place spoonfuls of the mixture on it, spaced well apart.

Bake for about 25 minutes, or until the macaroons are lightly colored. Allow them to cool before removing them from the parchment paper. Serve the cookies immediately, or store them in an airtight container.

Ernesto Stelle
Gallo d'Oro
Sassari, Italy

Biscotti

(Cookies)

Yield: 4 dozen small cookies

2 egg yolks
1/2 teaspoon vanilla extract
2 1/4 cups all-purpose flour
3/4 cup sugar
1/4 teaspoon salt
1/4 cup butter, cut into bits
1/4 teaspoon grated orange zest
1 egg, beaten
Decoration: Maraschino cherries, pine nuts, cinnamon sugar, ginger sugar, plain coarse sugar, sliced candied fruit, or chopped nuts (almonds, cashews, pecans, pistachios, or walnuts)

Beat together the egg yolks and vanilla extract.

Sift together the flour, sugar, and salt onto a pastry board or into a bowl. Make a well in the center of the mound, and place in it the butter, orange zest, and combined egg yolks and vanilla. With your fingers, quickly work these ingredients into the flour to produce a thick, smooth dough. Shape the dough into a ball, wrap it in waxed paper, and chill it for 30 minutes.

Preheat the oven to 350°F.

Roll the dough to a thickness of 1/4 inch and cut out rounds about 2 1/2 inches in diameter. Brush them with the beaten egg and decorate them with one of the suggested decorations listed above.

Arrange the cookies on a cookie sheet. Bake for 12 minutes, or until they are lightly browned. Remove them to a rack to cool.

Variations

For Chocolate Biscotti, blend 1 1/2 ounces semisweet chocolate, melted and cooled, into the dough before cutting it. For Almond Biscotti, substitute almond extract for the vanilla extract.

Louis and Louise Dolceacqua
Hamden, Connecticut

Biscotti al'Anici

(Anise cookies)

Yield: 24 to 42 small cookies

1 cup sugar
1 cup butter
3 eggs
3 cups all-purpose flour
2 1/2 teaspoons baking powder
6 to 8 drops anise oil, or 3 to 4 drops anise oil and 3 to 4 drops vanilla extract

Preheat the oven to 375°F. Grease two 9-inch by 5-inch loaf pans.

In a large bowl, cream together the sugar and butter. Add the eggs and mix until smooth. Sift the flour and baking powder together, and stir them into the egg and sugar mixture. Stir in the anise oil (and vanilla extract, if desired). Knead until the dough is smooth.

Divide the dough into 2 parts, then form each part into an oblong loaf 3 inches wide and 3/4 inch thick. Place the loaves in the greased pans and bake for 15 minutes, or until a cake tester inserted in the center comes out clean.

Remove the pans from the oven and let the loaves cool slightly. Then remove the loaves from the pans and cut them into 1-inch crosswise slices. Place the slices on the greased baking sheets and toast them for 1 to 2 minutes on the lowest shelf under the broiler, watching carefully and turning until each side is lightly browned.

Anna Dolceacqua Carangelo
Santa Barbara, California

Italian Creams

Yield: About 3 dozen

A white fudge candy.

1 cup milk
3 cups sugar
1 1/2 teaspoons butter
1 teaspoon vanilla extract
3/4 cup chopped walnuts

Butter a large baking pan.

Heat the milk and 2 cups of the sugar in a large, heavy saucepan, stirring occasionally. Allow the mixture to boil gently. Add the butter.

While the milk mixture heats, heat the remaining sugar in a heavy skillet, stirring gently so the sugar melts without burning. When the sugar in the skillet is completely melted, remove the hot milk and sugar mixture from the heat and stir the melted sugar into it. Return the saucepan to the heat and cook, stirring gently, until the temperature reaches 234°F, or when a drop of the mixture placed in water forms a soft ball. Remove the pan from the heat, and beat the mixture by hand until it thickens. Add the vanilla extract and walnuts. Pour the candy into the buttered pan and let it cool. When it is firm, cut it into squares as you would fudge.

Roger Smith and Laura Noel
Palm Springs, California

Sources of Italian Foods and Cooking Equipment

Italian Groceries

Durum wheat flour, fresh virgin olive oil, imported cheeses, imported dry pastas, sausages, sun-dried tomatoes packed in oil, etc.

Dean & Deluca
560 Broadway, Suite 304
New York, NY 10012
NY: (212) 432-1691
Elsewhere: (800) 221-7714
Call or write for a free catalog; they sell a variety of imported and domestic specialty foods.

G. B. Ratto & Co.
International Grocers
821 Washington Street
Oakland, CA 94607
CA: (800) 228-3515
Elsewhere (800) 325-3483
Call or write for a free catalog; they sell a variety of imported and domestic specialty foods.

Il Conte Di Savoia
555 West Roosevelt Road
Chicago, IL 60607

Manganaro Foods
488 9th Ave.
New York, NY 10018

Paprikas Weiss
1546 2nd Ave.
New York, NY 10021

Riviera Italian Foods
3220 North Harlem Ave.
Harwood Heights, IL 60656

Todaro Brothers
555 2nd Ave.
New York, NY 10016

Italian Cooking Equipment

Pizza pans, baking stones, baker's peels, pasta rollers, etc.

El Molina Mills
345 North Baldwin Park
City of Industry, CA

Foley Manufacturing Company
Housewares Division
330 Northeast 5th St.
Minneapolis, MN

Sassafras Enterprises, Inc.
PO Box 1366
Evanston, IL 60204

Williams-Sonoma
PO Box 7456
San Francisco, CA 94120

INDEX